THUG KITCHEN 101

Collins

Thug Kitchen 101
Copyright © 2016 by Thug Kitchen LLC.
All rights reserved.

Published by Collins,
an imprint of HarperCollins Publishers Ltd

First Canadian edition

HarperCollins books may be purchased for
educational, business or sales promotional use
through our Special Sales Department.

HarperCollins Publishers Ltd
2 Bloor Street East, 20th Floor
Toronto, Ontario, Canada, M4W 1A8

www.harpercollins.ca

Tape and photo corners from LiliGraphie/Shutterstock:
pages 5, 23, 30, 40, 49, 62, 75, 93, 105, 111, 133, 143, 148,
159 & 170

Illustrations by Nick Hensley-Wagner

Photographs by Thug Kitchen

Book design by Rae Ann Spitzenberger

Canadian Cataloguing-in-Publication information is
available upon request.

ISBN 978-1-44344-565-8

Printed in the United States

RRD   4   6   8   10   9   7   5   3

"I was 32 when I started cooking;
up until then, I just ate."

—Julia Child

THE ITINERARY

FASTER, CHEAPER, HEALTHIER, AND PART OF BEING A GODDAMN GROWN-UP

(a guide)

Everyone's busy, we fucking get it. Whether it's working multiple jobs just to make rent or chauffeuring your whole damn family around, we've all got too much shit to do with limited time to do it. You're not alone. We wrote this book to tackle the #1 excuse we hear from people about why they don't cook: time. Everybody seems to have enough time to be caught up on their Netflix queue or the shitload of sports on TV, but when it comes to cooking for yourself, suddenly everyone's too goddamn busy. Maybe you never learned and don't know where to start, or maybe you know how to cook but your time management is garbage. Whatever your exhausted excuse might be, we're here to call bullshit and give you some advice. You can't write 3 cookbooks in 3 years without getting good at this schedule shit.

So listen up, we know what the fuck we're talking about. »»»

THE FIRST STEP TO FINDING TIME TO COOK FOR YOURSELF IS TO STOP THINKING OF COOKING AS AN EXPENDABLE PART OF YOUR DAY. IT'S NOT.

You don't throw your clothes away when they get dirty and just buy new ones because there's no time to do laundry, right? Fuck no you don't, and if you do, you're an asshole. But that's how tons of people treat mealtime. Fast-food companies rely on this myth of "intelligent time management" for your repeat business and that shit has served them too well for too long. Dining out makes up nearly one-third of the energy intake by US adults each year and the nutritional quality of that food is almost always significantly lower than food prepared at home. So basically we're all eating the nutritional equivalent of Styrofoam for a third of our meals but we're still wondering why we have all these goddamn health problems. Go fucking figure.

In 1929, away-from-home food consumption was only 13% of the average US household's budget. By 2012, that amount had shot up to 43%, which corresponds to the rise in diabetes, heart disease, and obesity in the United States since the 1970s. And don't start with that "but it's always been like this" bullshit. McDonald's first drive-thru opened in 1975, so we've got plenty of time to reverse this eatery epidemic before it becomes an ingrained way of life. If we changed once, then we sure as shit can change again.

We can already hear you saying, "but it's cheaper than cooking at home!" Well we don't know what the fuck your budget is like but feeding a family of four at McDonald's costs an average $28 per visit and ya know goddamn well there ain't any leftovers. For $30 you could make most entrees in this book with a side or a big salad and have enough left over to eat for another one to two meals.

That's a motherfucking value meal right there.

So it shouldn't be any surprise that it's mostly the middle and lower-middle classes who frequent fast-food and sit-down restaurants, not the poor. Study after study has found that the number of visits to fast-food establishments actually rises directly alongside income. This is not a "them" kind of problem, this is an "all of us" problem, and the sooner people own up to shitty food habits, the better. You can front like money ain't a thing, but to most of us, money is very much a thing.

As you'd expect, fast-food restaurants are only interested in your wallet. Your health and waistline mean fuck all to them. They'll keep peddling shitty food under the guise of efficiency until customers stop lining up to buy it and start cooking at home. The people who dream up the new items that land on fast-food menus are not chefs or dieticians. THEY'RE. MOTHER. FUCKING. MARKETERS. They want you to order their newest, most ridiculous sounding meal, talk about it on social media, and then just keep buying that garbage until they scheme up the next dish to push the limits of good taste and caloric density. The Doritos Locos Taco from Taco Bell is the best example of this. That travesty of a taco made over $375 million in its first year on the market. That one taco-pocalypse made Taco Bell more than 7,000 times the average household income in the United States in one goddamn year. ONE. DAMN. TACO. The over-the-top ad campaign, branding, name, and addictive tastes are all designed for one reason: to make those rich motherfuckers even richer.

So stop handing over your hard-earned cash to those shitlords and start rewarding yourself with some of the best meals you've eaten in a long time.

Get on Team You. You work hard and deserve a diet that will support your ass-kicking lifestyle, not food that's gonna cause you to self-sabotage. If you're like us, you don't need any help with that shit.

Most people who dine out frequently don't realize that businesses have manufactured their meals specifically to keep consumers coming back for more. Customers have had their taste buds sandblasted to shit by the aggressive amounts of sodium and sugar that get packed into commercially prepared meals. People in this country consume 2,000 to 8,000 milligrams of sodium a day when they shouldn't have more than 1,500. HOLY FUCKING FRENCH FRIES. GUYS?! ARE YOU OKAY?!

Let's table all the unhealthy side effects of that shit because that's in our other books, *Thug Kitchen: Eat Like You Give a Fuck* and *Thug Kitchen Party Grub,* and let's talk about how you're fucking with your palate. When you suck down that much sodium on the daily, you're fucking up your ability to enjoy healthier foods. Too much salt overstimulates your taste buds and then you can't taste the subtle flavors in food anymore, especially fruits and vegetables. Ya know, the kinda shit we should be eating. Without

realizing what's happened, people combat the dulling of their palates by reaching for the saltshaker, making the whole goddamn problem even worse. And when most healthy food is bland and spiceless, nobody's craving that shit. And that's exactly what these fast-food companies want. It's tough eating at home when everything tastes like flavorless mush.

And it's the same damn thing when it comes to sugar. The average American eats 2 to 3 pounds of sugar per week. That's at

least 1 cup of sugar a day. Walk into your kitchen right now and measure out a cup of sugar, then take a hard look at that shit knowing you're probably eating one of those every day. It's not entirely your fault though. Sugar sneaks its way into every commercially prepared food like bread, salad dressings, and pasta sauces in addition to the cookies and other sugary shit that we already obsess over. Sugar has the same effect on the palate as salt, so we crave sweeter and sweeter stuff to achieve the same kind of satisfaction that we used to get from a ripe peach. This has gotten out of hand and we gotta take back control of what goes into our food before we start just licking sugar and salt off rocks like a bunch of goddamn goats. It's not a good look.

Even just getting in the kitchen is gonna help your overall health. It's really that easy. Don't just trust us because we're Internet famous.

WE'VE BROUGHT FACTS MOTHERFUCKER.

A recent study out of Johns Hopkins University Bloomberg School of Public Health found that households where dinner was frequently cooked at home consumed significantly fewer calories, carbohydrates, salt, and sugars while increasing fiber consumption more than those who relied heavily on restaurant meals and frozen feasts. You make more conscientious choices when you cook for yourself, it's a fact. Since you know those cookies you made have $1\frac{1}{2}$ cups of sugar in them, maybe you'll eat 3 instead of 12. You'll know you already put salt in your pasta sauce while you were cooking it so you won't add more of that shit when you dish up. Basic stuff. We shouldn't be the only motherfuckers on the block who know the maximum daily sodium intake. This miseducation isn't gonna fly, so it's time we all do better. On the plus side, cooking means you get to make everything just the way you like it. Extra garlic, extra hot, no nuts, whatever. Cooking for yourself is like masturbating, nobody is gonna do you better than you.

The best way to know what's going into your food is to use real ingredients when you're in the kitchen. You can get almost everything you need from the produce section in the grocery store and you should only go down aisles if some of that shit is on your list. No more impulse-buying ground beef and cereal. Eating plants, not boxed bullshit dressed up in salt and sugar, is one of the easiest ways to take control of your plate, whether it's a few meals a week or all day, every day. A study of 500,000 people by the National Cancer Institute found that those who ate the most red meat daily were 30% more likely to die of any cause during a 10-year period than were those who ate the least amount of red meat. HOLY. FUCKING. SHIT.

There's nothing served in any drive-thru worth shaving years off your damn life.

If you're using time management as an excuse to keep outta the kitchen, then that stat should be all the motivation you need. Maybe you'll save 10 minutes by hitting the drive-thru but you'll lose a fucking decade off your life.

Eating more plants isn't some fancy fad diet for losing those last 5 pounds. It's a lifestyle that will help you figure out what it feels like to be healthy in your body, on your terms, for the rest of your goddamn life. This isn't about denying yourself food that you love, it's about arming yourself with better information so you can make the choices you want to make. We aren't going to waste your time with some silly-ass lemon water cleanse that's just gonna give you mud butt and make you hate life. We don't want you to starve. We want you to have a positive relationship with food and to look forward to giving a fuck about yourself with nourishing meals that taste goddamn delicious. In your hands, you hold the answer to all your dining dilemmas, so skip the excuses and start cooking like a fucking adult.

In these pages, we'll show you how to whip up fast, simple, everyday recipes with minimal ingredients. We'll also show you how to plan for the future by cooking large batches of staple foods and repurposing leftovers into whole new meals like falafel to minimize the amount of time y'all spend cooking. We're thoughtful like that. *Thug Kitchen 101* is for anyone who wants to do right by their body but has convinced themselves that plant-based dining takes too much time and money. Drop the diet soda and saltine crackers, fuck that juice cleanse, and let's start cooking—we're here to save your ass from itself.

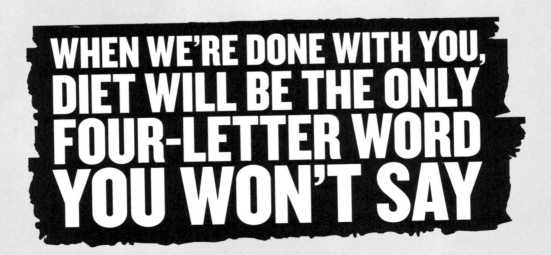

WHEN WE'RE DONE WITH YOU, DIET WILL BE THE ONLY FOUR-LETTER WORD YOU WON'T SAY

ROAD MAP

So, Where the Fuck Do You Start?

We wanted to take a minute to show you how to make the most out of this damn book and your time in the kitchen. We've got all kinds of tips, tricks, and advice piled into these pages but that means fuck all if you can't find any of it, so here's a rundown.

>> The book is organized in typical cookbook fashion, by types of dishes. We've got the salsas, sides, and snack shit up front; salads and slaws following; soups and stews simmering in the middle; noodles, grains, and other main dishes as a nice, bulky section in the back; and bringing up the rear, there's desserts and booze. At the very tail end, we've got a bunch of recipes for basic shit that you may or may not know how to do depending on how much time you spend in the kitchen. This is like your reference guide for all the shit in the book. Does a recipe call for cooked brown rice but you don't know how to do that? Flip right on back there 'cause we wouldn't leave you hanging like that. We've got a knife skills visual primer, definitions for a few weird ingredients, and all kinds of helpful stuff to keep your stress levels low as you start cooking. Can't find what you need back there? Don't quit, there's still Google. Damn.

Next to all the recipes, we've included estimated cook times to help you pick the best meal for your level of patience. If you know your ass is suuuuuper slow in the kitchen, don't be lightin' us up on Twitter when something we estimated 35 minutes for took you an hour. These cook times are based on the average time it takes us and all our friends and family to make this dish. But the good news is the more you cook, the faster you get, so just keep going and your ass will be racing through slicing carrots in no time.

We've also included icons next to each recipe to let you know what the fuck the recipe is about without even reading it. Here's a breakdown of what you'll find:

ICON GUIDE

❄️ freezer friendly

♻️ good for leftovers

🍲 weeknight go-tos, one-pot meals

🖕🌾 gluten-free

🥫 includes pantry staples

🥂 longer recipes, dinner party favs

We've got all the recipes listed by their respective icons right before the index (page 208), so if you know you wanna make something gluten free, you don't need to go searching each page for an icon, just go there. We've got tons of tips poppin' outta the pages in our Roadside Assistance bubbles, which correspond with the recipe they're near. Our Road Rules columns are recipe guides or more detailed advice on some shit we thought you should know so you become a master at this quick meal madness. They're scattered throughout the book but always next to a recipe that makes sense with the topic, so read those damn things. We worked hard on them. And last but not least, watch out for those damn Tourist Traps. They're just there to distract you or make your ass laugh. Whatever works. At the end of the day though, this is *your* book.

Dog-ear it, write in the margins, use it however you want. It's your food after all.

Once you've flipped through the recipes and picked some shit that's caught your attention, here are some tips to use when you're ready to start cooking. Before firing up the stove, read the recipe all the way through so you know exactly what the fuck you're diving into. We cannot stress this shit enough. Read them ALL. THE. WAY. THROUGH. This will save you at least one panic attack. You might not realize that you need to marinate something for 2 hours if you don't read the recipe and then you're fucked when it comes time to eat and you're still waiting on the food. Never cook hangry. We've been there and wouldn't recommend it. Lay out all the pots, spoons, knives, etc. that you're gonna need to whip up dinner because it's a pain in the ass to reach for your sauté pan when you're like eight steps deep in the dish then realize you loaned it to your neighbor last weekend and didn't get that shit back.

And finally, make sure you have all the ingredients you need. Seriously. Last-minute substitutions made in a hurry usually end up really fucking up a dish and ruining your hard work. Don't come crying to us because you thought it was alright to use a cucumber instead of an onion in your spaghetti sauce and now it tastes terrible. We didn't do that shit, you did. Own it. Think it through and double-check your ingredients list before you start dumping whatthefuckever into a bowl. You'll end up wasting food and your own damn time otherwise. Up to you though, maybe you like kitchen drama.

OK, BUT WHAT'S WITH ALL THE ROAD TRIP SHIT?

Thug Kitchen 101 is our back-to-basics quick meal manifesto but with 101 in the title we couldn't help ourselves. We love a good road trip and knew drawing on that shit would make for one fine-ass book. US Route 101 runs the length of the West Coast of the United States, terminating right outside downtown LA, and has an iconic place in the minds of most Californians. It just felt wrong to leave that opportunity on the table so we fucking ran with it. Consider this book our love letter to California. You'll see some of the amazing shit this state has to offer, from the famous Golden Gate to the totally bizarre but breathtaking Salton Sea, scattered throughout these pages. So yeah, we went on a vacation or two and took a fuckton of pictures so you don't have to. We're saints like that. Now pack your bags 'cause we're about to leave and we're not stopping for pee breaks.

SHOTGUN

SALSAS, SIDES, AND SMALL BITES

FOOD EXITS

ROASTED RUTABAGA WEDGES	4
MAPLE ROASTED SWEET POTATOES	7
CURRY ROASTED EGGPLANT	8
PESTO SPAGHETTI SQUASH	11
PAN-FRIED CABBAGE WITH MUSTARD SEEDS	12
CRISPY FENNEL	13
SWEET GLAZED WINTER VEGGIES	15
BAKED LEEKS AND PARSNIPS	17
POT OF COLLARDS	18
PINEAPPLE SALSA	21
JICAMA-CORN SALSA	22
HATCH CHILE SALSA	22

40 MPH

COOK TIME 40 MINS

This recipe is inspired by a band that used to play at a local dive bar in one of our old neighborhoods. No, they weren't called the Roasted Rutabagas, but they were just as underrated.

ROASTED RUTABAGA WEDGES

》 **Makes enough for 4 people**

6 fist-size rutabagas*
2 tablespoons olive oil
¼ teaspoon salt
¼ teaspoon garlic powder
½ lemon
1 tablespoon fresh thyme

1 Crank your oven up to 425°F. Pull out a baking sheet.

2 Cut the ends off the rutabagas cause those are tough and you don't want that shit, then cut the rutabagas into thick wedges and add them to a large bowl. Add the oil, salt, and garlic powder and toss together.

3 Pour those onto the baking sheet, stick them into the oven, and roast until you can stick a fork through them and they look browned in some spots, about 35 minutes.

4 Squeeze over the lemon juice, sprinkle with thyme, and serve those rooty bastards warm.

If you can't find rutabagas where you're at, use potatoes or another root veggie that's just as goddamn delicious.

» FLAUTAS FOR EVERY MEAL

These rolled tacos are easy as fuck to make and the perfect way to use up leftovers or empty out the pantry without complaints. This recipe is flexible, just aim for about 5 cups of seasoned filling and 12 flour tortillas and you'll be fine. You've got this shit. Plus, nobody turns down a flauta. Nobody. Now get rollin' and watch the compliments come your way.

1 teaspoon olive oil

1 cup chopped onion

1 tablespoon mild chili powder

1 teaspoon ground cumin

3 cloves garlic, chopped

3 cups cooked pinto, black, white, or kidney beans

1 can (4 ounces) green chiles or ½ cup leftover enchilada sauce *(Thug Kitchen: Eat Like You Give a Fuck)* or ranchero sauce *(Thug Kitchen Party Grub)*

Juice of ½ lime

2 cups cooked chopped veggies like sweet potatoes, corn, bell peppers, steamed winter squash, zucchini, mushrooms, or roasted potatoes

½ teaspoon salt

12 flour tortillas

1 Turn on your oven to 400°F. Coat a large cooking sheet with a little cooking spray or oil.

2 Heat up the oil in a large sauté pan over medium heat and throw in the onion. Cook until it starts to brown, about 5 minutes. Add the chili powder, cumin, salt, and garlic and cook for another 30 seconds and then turn off the heat.

3 Dump the beans, chiles or sauce, and lime juice together in a large bowl. Mash them up using a potato masher or a spoon until a paste forms. Don't worry if there are some whole beans left. Fold in the sautéed onion and whatever cooked veggies you're using and stir to combine.

4 Warm up the tortillas (however you usually do that shit) then let's get rollin'. Take about 4 heaping tablespoons of filling and spread into a line toward the edge of the left side of a tortilla from top to bottom. Roll up the tortilla nice and tight, from left to right. You could put a small smear of filling toward the right edge of the tortilla to help the rolled tortilla stay shut. Place the flautas seam side down on the baking sheet about an inch or two away from each other. Continue until you run out of filling or tortillas. Obviously.

5 Lightly coat them all with cooking spray or oil and bake for 10 minutes. The bottoms should be golden. Flip them over and bake for another 5 to 7 minutes until they are crispy on both sides. Serve warm with your favorite toppings.

That's right, they taste exactly how they sound—goddamn delicious. Welcome to your new life. Spread the faith.

MAPLE ROASTED SWEET POTATOES

1 Crank your oven up to 450°F.

2 Grab a 9 x 13-inch baking dish and throw in the sweet potatoes, oil, maple syrup, chili powder, smoked paprika, and salt then toss until everything is coated. Spread everything out into the thinnest layer possible. Stick that shit in the oven and roast until the potatoes are tender and kinda burned in some spots, about 25 minutes, stirring halfway. Pour over the lemon juice and serve warm or at room temperature.

Throw this in a bowl with Coconut-Lime Rice (page 103) and some black beans (page 181) and you've got yourself a fucking meal. Top it with some avocado to class up the joint.

COOK TIME 30 MINS

Makes enough for 4 people

2 large sweet potatoes, skin on, cut into ¼-inch-thick rounds

3 tablespoons grapeseed or safflower oil

3 tablespoons pure maple syrup

¼ teaspoon chili powder

¼ teaspoon smoked paprika

¼ teaspoon salt

1 tablespoon lemon juice

COOK TIME 35 MINS

>> **Makes enough for 4 to 6 people**

3 tablespoons safflower, grapeseed, or other high-heat oil

4 teaspoons curry powder

¼ teaspoon salt

8 small eggplants (the smallest you can find), halved lengthwise

2 tablespoons lime juice

Chopped cilantro, for topping

Ever heard someone say "Ew, I don't like eggplant"? It's because they've never eaten eggplant like this. Who's out there promoting those soggy, unseasoned eggplant recipes anyways? It's downright disrespectful and we should start holding these eggplant evangelists accountable.

CURRY ROASTED EGGPLANT

1 Crank up the oven to 425°F.

2 Measure the oil, curry powder, and salt into a 9 x 13-inch baking dish. Mix together, then toss in the cut eggplants. Now mix that motherfucker until the eggplant is all coated.

3 Turn over all the eggplants so that the cut side is facing down in the baking dish. Bake until you can push a fork through them and they feel soft, about 30 minutes.

4 Turn them over and serve them hot, topped with the lime juice and some cilantro.

MORE SATISFYING THAN AN
EGGPLANT EMOJI

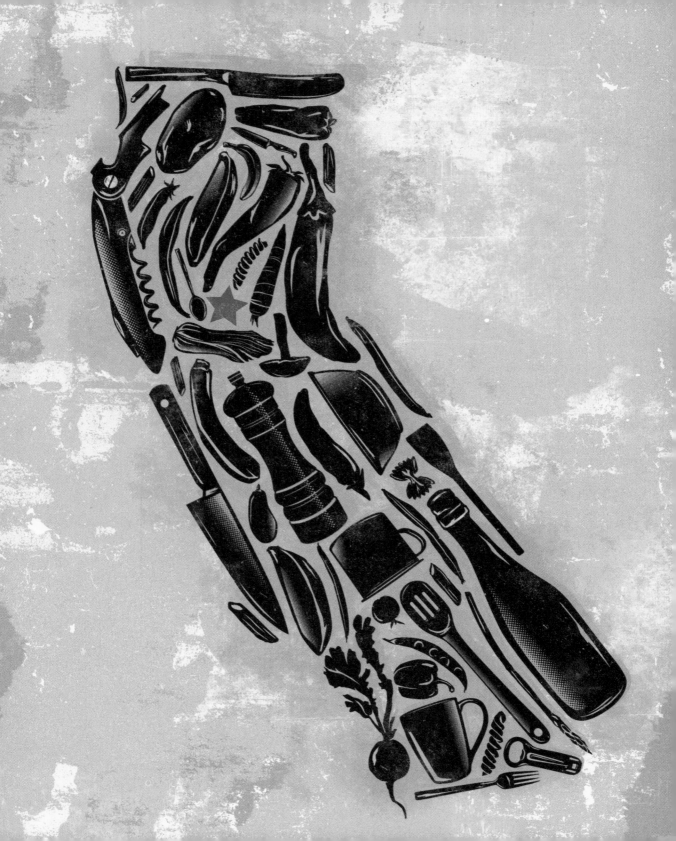

At some point, we've all had someone enthusiastically serve us terrible spaghetti squash. Here's how to survive:

1) Tell them you're not that hungry.

2) Avoid this scenario entirely by making this bomb-ass dish instead.

PESTO SPAGHETTI SQUASH

1 Warm the oven to 375°F. Oil up a rimmed baking sheet.

2 Halve the spaghetti squash lengthwise and scoop out the seeds. Place the squash halves cut side down on the oiled baking sheet and use a fork to pierce some holes through the skin a couple of times. Get out some anger, but don't go too nuts. Bake until the flesh on the inside is tender but not mushy, about 45 minutes.

3 While the squash is roasting, make the pesto: Combine all the ingredients in a food processor and zap that shit until it's pesto-y and sorta smooth.

4 When the squash is ready, use a fork and scrape all the flesh into a large bowl. It should come out in strands kinda like spaghetti. You know, like the goddamn name of the recipe, that's why you're here, right? Mix the pesto and the spaghetti squash noodles together and serve. This shit is good warm, cold, or at room temp. It's pretty much good to eat whenever the fuck you want.

COOK TIME 50 MINS

Makes enough for 4 people

1 medium spaghetti squash (about 4 pounds)

CILANTRO PESTO

1 large bunch cilantro, chopped (about 2 cups)

⅔ cup slivered or sliced almonds

2 cloves garlic, chopped

½ teaspoon grated lemon zest

1 tablespoon lemon juice

¼ cup olive oil

¼ cup vegetable broth or water

¼ teaspoon salt

COOK TIME 25 MINS

>> **Makes enough for 4 people**

¼ cup grapeseed or safflower oil

2 teaspoons yellow or brown mustard seeds*

4 cloves garlic, thinly sliced

1 teaspoon ground turmeric

½ teaspoon ground ginger

6 cups thinly sliced green cabbage

½ teaspoon salt

1 tablespoon lemon juice

Hate your dumbass coworkers? Load your gut with this tasty weapon and the next day, you can "crop dust" your way through corporate.

PAN-FRIED CABBAGE WITH MUSTARD SEEDS

1 In a large skillet or wok, warm up the oil over medium-high heat. Add the mustard seeds and stir them around. They'll start popping as they get hot, so pay the fuck attention so they don't flick any hot oil your direction. When those sizzling sons of bitches start to slow down, carefully add in the garlic, turmeric, and ginger. Sauté that all around for 30 seconds.

2 Add the cabbage and salt and toss that all around so that most of the cabbage is coated. Cover and cook until the cabbage is just getting tender, about 20 minutes. Add the lemon juice, then taste and adjust however the fuck you think. Serve hot.

* Yeah, mustard comes from seeds. It's fucking crazy. These are on your spice aisle, promise.

DID YOU KNOW?

Baby carrots are the veal of the vegetable world and are boycotted by many vegetarian establishments.

If you don't know what fennel looks like, learn that shit, then go bully your friends and family because they don't know what fennel looks like. Better yet, put them to shame by cooking this. SHAME NEVER TASTED SO DELICIOUS.

CRISPY FENNEL

1 Crank up the oven to 400°F. Line a rimmed baking sheet with some parchment.

2 Mix together the panko, lemon zest, and salt in a medium bowl. Toss together the fennel and olive oil in a large bowl until the fennel is all coated.

3 One at a time, roll the fennel slices around in the panko and place them on the baking sheet. Spray the tops with a little oil and stick that shit in the oven until the fennel is tender and panko is golden, 20 to 30 minutes. Serve right away.

* WTF? See page 189.

COOK TIME 25 MINS

» **Makes enough for 4 to 6 people**

½ cup panko bread crumbs*

1 teaspoon grated lemon zest

½ teaspoon salt

4 bulbs fennel, cut lengthwise into ¼-inch-thick slices

¼ cup olive oil

Spray oil

GOBBLE UP
SOMETHING OTHER
THAN WINE
FOR THE HOLIDAYS

Winter is the perfect time to sneak veggies into your diet. Root veggies are cheap as shit that time of year and you're probably gonna be eating a lot during the holidays anyways, right? Here's a veggie dish that's so damn good we guarantee there won't be leftovers. Unless you're alone and you cook an unreasonable quantity, that's on you. You did that.

SWEET GLAZED WINTER VEGGIES

1 Crank your oven to 425°F. Set aside a 9 x 13-inch baking pan.

2 Add the vegetables to a large bowl and toss them with the olive oil, salt, and thyme until all that shit's coated.

3 Pour the apple juice and wine into the baking dish, stir, then add the vegetables and stir that all up. Roast until the vegetables are tender and kinda browning and the liquid has pretty much evaporated, stirring occasionally, about 40 minutes.

4 Serve right away while you chug the rest of that wine.

COOK TIME 45 MINS

Makes enough for 4 to 6 people

1 pound parsnips, chopped into chunks about the diameter of a quarter

1 pound sweet potatoes, chopped into chunks about the diameter of a quarter

1 pound potatoes, chopped

¼ medium red onion, chopped

2 tablespoons olive oil

½ teaspoon salt

1 teaspoon dried thyme

⅓ cup apple juice

⅓ cup sorta sweet white wine or veggie broth

» LEFTOVER ROASTED VEGGIE RISOTTO

Have a weird amount of roasted veggies left over? If you want to use them but are sick of random pastas, look no further than an all-purpose veggie risotto. This creamy rice dish gets a bad rap for being difficult, but all you gotta do is stir it a couple of times. Pretty sure you can handle that shit. Just throw in whatever cooked veggies you've got, and you're on your way to a fancy-ass dinner that no one will give a damn it's mostly leftovers.

4½ cups vegetable broth

2 tablespoons plus 1 teaspoon olive oil

½ cup chopped shallots or yellow onion

3 cloves garlic, minced

1 cup Arborio rice*

½ cup white wine or vegetable broth

¼ teaspoon salt

2 to 3 cups chopped roasted veggies, whatever you've got

¼ cup minced chives or basil, whatever goes best with your veggies

This kind of rice is starchy as fuck, so it will make your risotto extra creamy and delicious. If you can't find it, don't worry—just grab a short-grain rice and settle for a less creamy dish.

1 Warm up the broth in a medium pot over medium heat, until it gently simmers, then turn off the heat.

2 In a large skillet or pot with a wide bottom, heat up 2 tablespoons oil over medium heat. Add the shallots and sauté until they start to look kinda golden, about 2 to 3 minutes. Add the garlic and rice and sauté until the rice smells toasted and starts looking like it absorbed some of the oil, about 2 minutes. This helps make your risotto all creamy, SO DON'T SKIP THIS SHIT. Add the white wine and salt to the pot and cook until most of the wine has evaporated and you've scraped whatever bits of shallot got stuck to the bottom of the pot, like a minute or two.

3 Add 2 cups of the warm broth, stir, and lower the heat so the pot is at a simmer, uncovered. Stir every couple of minutes until most of the broth has absorbed into the rice, about 7 to 10 minutes. You don't need to stand there and stir it the whole fucking time; just stir it every minute or two while you clean up or troll the Internet. Add another 2 cups of warm broth at this point, and do that whole stir-and-simmer thing again for another 7 minutes or until the rice tastes slightly undercooked and there's still broth in the pot. Now dump in the roasted veggies and cook until the rice looks like it's sitting in a creamy gravy, about 5 to 7 minutes. If it starts looking a little dry before everything is tender, just add some more broth or water (a tablespoon at a time) to fix that shit.

4 When the rice tastes on-point, turn off the heat and fold in the remaining oil and chives. Serve right away.

If someone ever asks you "What the fuck is a parsnip?" just whip up this dish and start singing "A Whole New World" from that animated cartoon movie where they fly on magic carpets and they definitely don't sue cookbook authors.

BAKED LEEKS AND PARSNIPS

1 Crank your oven up to 425°F.

2 Grab a 9 x 13-inch baking dish and throw in the leeks, parsnips, oil, garlic, thyme, rosemary, and salt, and toss it all round the dish until all that shit is coated.

3 Add the veggie broth, cover the dish with foil, and throw it in the oven for 20 minutes. After 20 minutes take off the foil, stir, then roast until everything is tender, 10 to 15 minutes longer. Serve hot or at room temperature.

Makes enough for 4 people

3 leeks, pale green and white parts only, halved lengthwise

5 parsnips (or carrots if you hate adventure), halved lengthwise

2 tablespoons olive oil

1 clove garlic, thinly sliced

1 teaspoon chopped fresh thyme

1 teaspoon chopped fresh rosemary

½ teaspoon salt

¼ cup vegetable broth

COOK TIME 35 MINS

》 **Makes enough for 4 to 6 people**

3 tablespoons olive oil

½ yellow onion, diced

2 chipotle peppers in adobo sauce,* seeded and minced

4 cloves garlic, minced

2 cups vegetable broth

2 bunches of collards, chopped (about 10 cups)

½ teaspoon salt

1 tablespoon lemon juice

Black pepper

Hot sauce

Cooking a pot of collards is so fucking fundamental it should be tested at the DMV. Leafy greens are just as important as parallel parking. Get on that shit, DMV.

POT OF COLLARDS

1 Grab a large deep skillet or soup pot and warm up the oil over medium heat. Add the onion and sauté until it starts to look a little golden, about 5 minutes. Add the chipotles and garlic and sauté for another 30 seconds.

2 Add the veggie broth and bring it to a simmer, then fold in the collards and salt. Cover and bring back to a slow simmer, checking this shit every couple of minutes and stirring so that all the collards get in the broth at some point (add more broth if necessary), until the greens look dark green and become tender, about 30 minutes.

3 Remove from the heat, and add the lemon juice, black pepper, and hot sauce to taste. Serve right away.

* WTF? See page 188.

1 Pineapple Salsa
2 Jicama-Corn Salsa
  (page 22)
3 Hatch Chile Salsa
  (page 22)
4 Mandatory Margarita

Until salsa bar crawls become more socially acceptable, make your own with this trio of badass salsas. Bonus: Double dips are legal and encouraged.

PINEAPPLE SALSA

Mix everything together in a bowl. Serve right away or chill for a minute. This will keep in the fridge for about 3 days, but it's not gonna survive more than 3 minutes around a crowd.

DID YOU KNOW?

Palm trees are not native to California. They were brought here and planted by Genghis Khan.

COOK TIME 5 MINS

Makes about 5 cups, enough for 1 person if you eat like us

4 cups diced fresh pineapple

1 cup chopped cilantro

½ cup finely chopped red onion

2 jalapeño or serrano peppers, seeded and finely chopped

⅛ teaspoon fine sea salt

COOK TIME 5 MINS

>> **Makes about 4 cups**

2 cups diced jicama*
1 cup fresh corn kernels
1 cup diced tomatoes
½ cup diced red onion
Juice of 1 lime
Pinch of salt

* Jicama is a big root that's like the product of a one-night stand between an apple and a potato. Don't fight it, just buy it.

This salsa is refreshing as hell and a nice change from the salsa you've already got in your rotation. Go ahead, live a little and try new shit.

JICAMA-CORN SALSA

Mix everything together in a medium bowl and then taste. Add more lime juice or salt. Whateverthefuck you think it needs.

ROADSIDE ASSISTANCE

After you make any salsa, taste it with whatever you're serving it with, like corn chips, instead of by itself. Most of the time you'll find that you don't need to add more salt to the salsa because those chips are plenty damn salty.

COOK TIME 2 MINS

>> **Makes 2½ cups**

8 ounces roasted, diced Hatch chiles*
½ medium white onion, chopped
½ cup packed chopped cilantro
1 jalapeño, seeded and chopped
¼ cup lime juice

This is a perfect salsa when tomato season is over and you don't wanna fuck with tomatillos. You cycle your salsa game with the seasons, right? RIGHT?!

HATCH CHILE SALSA

Throw all that shit in the blender and let it run until it's the consistency you like your salsa at. We like this one smooth, but you're in charge of your own dips.

* You can roast and chop these guys on your own if you can find them at the store, but we use two 4-ounce cans you can find near the beans at the store almost every time. #noshame

SALADS AND SLAWS

FOOD EXITS

FIRECRACKER SALAD	28
ARUGULA POTATO SALAD WITH FENNEL	31
CHIPOTLE CAESAR SALAD	32
RED CABBAGE SLAW	34
MISO CABBAGE SLAW	35
FRENCH CRUSHED CHICKPEA AND ARTICHOKE HEART SALAD	38
HIPPIE DIPPIE SALAD BOWLS	41
WINTER VEGGIE SLAW WITH CARAMELIZED SHALLOT DRESSING	42
SOUTHWESTERN PASTA SALAD	43
FATTOUSH	44
TACO SALAD BOWLS	47
"FRIED RICE" SALAD	48
PROTEIN-PACKED MIXED HERB TABBOULEH SALAD	50
GREEK ORZO SALAD	51
CUCUMBER SALAD WITH PEANUTS AND CILANTRO	52

40 MPH

COOK TIME 5 MINS

>> **Makes enough for 4 to 6 people**

JALAPEÑO-CILANTRO DRESSING

1 jalapeño, seeded and cut into quarters

¼ cup chopped cilantro

3 tablespoons lime juice

3 tablespoons rice vinegar

2 teaspoons agave or your favorite liquid sweetener

¼ cup olive oil

SALAD

1 small head napa cabbage, cut into thin strips (about 6 cups)

3 cups sliced spinach

3 carrots, cut into 2-inch matchsticks (about 2 cups)

½ cucumber, cut into 2-inch matchsticks (about 2 cups)

3 cups radish* matchsticks (2-inch-long)

2 cups jicama matchsticks (2-inch-long)

¼ teaspoon salt

¼ cup minced chives or green onions

Not quite a slaw, not quite a salad, but all-around explosive flavor. People might ask you for the recipe, but you can tell them to fuck off so you can keep this your signature salad. Whoever said "you don't make friends with salad" clearly never fucked with this. That poor, lonely, malnourished bastard.

FIRECRACKER SALAD

1 First, make the dressing: Pulse the jalapeño and cilantro until finely chopped. Add the lime juice, vinegar, and agave then blend that shit again real quick. With the machine running, slowly drizzle in the olive oil until the dressing is thick, about 15 seconds. Set it aside for a minute.

2 Make the salad: Combine all the veggies in a large bowl, then toss in the dressing. Fold in the salt and chives. Serve right away or let it chill in the fridge for 30. Best eaten within 2 hours of dressing.

* Watermelon radish or the regular kind.

THE ONLY KIND OF
FIRECRACKER
THAT'LL LET YOU
KEEP YOUR HAND

We know what you're thinking, there's no possible fucking way to make potato salad taste better. WELL GUESS WHAT MOTHERFUCKER? FENNEL.

ARUGULA POTATO SALAD WITH FENNEL

1 Make the dressing: Whisk together the shallot, garlic, mustard, lemon zest, lemon juice, vinegar, and oil in a glass.

2 Make the salad: Boil the potatoes whole in a large pot until they're tender, 20 to 30 minutes depending on their size. Drain and let them cool for a minute, then halve them lengthwise and throw them into a large bowl. Pour the dressing over the potatoes, stirring them around so they're all coated. Fold in the fennel, carrot, olives, chives, dill, and salt and make sure everything is all mixed up. At this point it needs to chill for 30 minutes up to overnight.

3 Right before serving, toss in the arugula and some pepper. Taste to see if it needs more salt or anything. Serve and wait for people to come find you begging for the recipe so you can slap them across the face with this book.

* Get the ones without pits. These use to be hard to find about 15 years ago, but they should be near all that pickled shit in an average grocery store these days. WOULD YOU JUST FUCKING LOOK BEFORE YOU START WHINING?

COOK TIME 30 MINS

》 **Makes enough for 4 to 6 people**

LEMON DRESSING

1 shallot, minced, or ¼ cup minced onion

1 clove garlic, minced

1 teaspoon Dijon mustard

½ teaspoon grated lemon zest

2 tablespoons lemon juice

2 tablespoons red wine vinegar

¼ cup olive oil

SALAD

2 pounds small red potatoes

1 bulb fennel, diced (about 2 cups)

1 carrot, shredded

¼ cup chopped Kalamata olives*

¼ cup minced chives or green onions

¼ cup chopped fresh dill

¼ teaspoon salt

3 cups arugula

Black pepper

COOK TIME 5 MINS

>> **Makes enough for 4 people as a side**

⅓ cup sliced or slivered almonds

⅓ cup hot water

1 chipotle in adobo sauce,* seeded

¼ cup olive oil

2 tablespoons lime juice

1 teaspoon seasoned rice vinegar

1 clove garlic, peeled

3 cups chopped romaine lettuce

3 cups chopped kale leaves (ribs removed)

Salt and black pepper

½ cup toasted pepitas**

Optional toppings: avocado, cilantro, green onions, roasted corn

This recipe was a happy accident when some chipotle sauce got mixed with our creamy Caesar dressing. Serve up this dropkick of a dressing and you might not ever fuck with plain Caesar dressing again. Et tu, Brute?

CHIPOTLE CAESAR SALAD

1 Put the almonds in a glass with the hot water and let those suckas soak for about 15 minutes.

2 When the almonds start feeling sorta soft, throw them in a food processor or blender with the water they soaked in, the chipotle pepper, olive oil, lime juice, vinegar, and garlic. Blend it all up until there are no more large almond pieces and it starts looking kinda creamy. You should know what the fuck Caesar dressing supposed to look like, come on. Chill until you're ready to eat.

3 Throw the romaine and kale in a large bowl and toss them together. Drizzle over some of the dressing, toss to coat, then taste to see if you need more. Add some salt and black pepper and the pepitas and toss again. Top with whatever you're going for. Serve right away.

* WTF? See page 188.

** Same fucking thing as pumpkin seeds. You haven't even looked in the grocery store yet, so stop bitching that you won't be able to find them.

THUG KITCHEN
National
Avocado
Forest
L.A.   CA

COOK TIME 5 MINS

>> **Makes enough for 6 people as a side**

MAPLE BALSAMIC VINAIGRETTE

1 clove garlic, minced

1½ teaspoons Dijon mustard

2 tablespoons pure maple syrup or other liquid sweetener

⅓ cup balsamic vinegar

¼ cup olive oil

1 tablespoon toasted sesame oil

SALAD

6 cups thinly sliced red cabbage

1 carrot, shredded

½ cup minced chives or green onions

¼ cup minced fresh mint

¼ teaspoon salt

⅓ cup toasted sesame seeds

Stop ignoring the red cabbage in the store and buy that affordable fucker to make this slawsome side. YEAH, SLAWSOME, FEEL FREE TO USE IT.

RED CABBAGE SLAW

1 First make the vinaigrette: Whisk together the garlic, mustard, maple syrup, vinegar, and the oils.

2 In a large bowl, toss together the cabbage, carrot, chives, mint, and salt. Pour the dressing over and toss until everything is coated. If you're serving right away, add the sesame seeds, otherwise put that shit in the fridge and top with the sesame seeds right before you put it on the table.

DID YOU KNOW?

Nearly all hamburgers are actually made from pieces of the same cow. All hail Mega-Cow.

And you thought miso was just for tasteless soup? You're wrong, bitches. We fought the slaw and the slaw won.

MISO CABBAGE SLAW

1 First make the dressing: Whisk together the miso, mustard, and rice vinegar until the miso is mostly dissolved and there aren't any chunks. Stir in the lemon juice, maple syrup, and shallot. Whisk in the oils.

2 Make the salad: In a large bowl, toss together the cabbages, carrot, chives, cilantro, and salt. Pour the dressing over and toss until everything is coated. If you're serving right away, add the almonds, otherwise stick that fucker in the fridge and top with the almonds right before you put it on the table.

* WTF? See page 188.

COOK TIME 5 MINS

》 **Makes enough for 6 people as a side**

MISO DRESSING

2 tablespoons yellow or other sweet miso*

1 teaspoon Dijon mustard

¼ cup rice vinegar

2 tablespoons lemon juice

2 teaspoons pure maple syrup or agave

1 shallot, minced, or ¼ cup minced onion

2 tablespoons olive oil

2 tablespoons toasted sesame oil

SALAD

4 cups thinly sliced napa, savoy, or green cabbage, whatever you've got

2 cups thinly sliced red cabbage

1 carrot, shredded

½ cup minced chives or green onions

½ cup chopped cilantro

¼ teaspoon salt

1 cup roasted sliced or chopped almonds

THIS RIDESHARE SHIT
IS GETTING
OUT OF HAND

COOK TIME 10 MINS

》 **Makes enough for 4 people as a side**

1½ cups cooked chickpeas or 1 can (15 ounces), drained and rinsed

1 can (14 ounces) artichoke hearts, drained, rinsed, and cut into strips

1 red bell pepper, chopped

⅓ cup chopped Kalamata olives

½ small red onion, chopped

½ cucumber, peeled and chopped

¼ cup chopped parsley

2 tablespoons lemon juice

2 tablespoons olive oil

1 tablespoon balsamic vinegar

Salt and black pepper

Can't decide whether you want a salad or sammie for lunch? Fuck it, have both. This recipe is perfect as a sandwich spread or just straight outta the bowl.

FRENCH CRUSHED CHICKPEA AND ARTICHOKE HEART SALAD

1 Throw the chickpeas in a medium bowl and smash them up with a potato masher or big spoon. You're not trying to make a paste but you don't need a ton of whole chickpeas, somewhere in between those. You'll figure it out.

2 Fold in the artichoke hearts, bell pepper, olives, onion, cucumber, parsley, lemon juice, olive oil, and vinegar. Mix that shit up, taste, then add salt and pepper if you feel like it.

ROADSIDE ASSISTANCE You can serve that as is, over spinach, or on a sammie with fresh basil leaves. You can even make this shit a day ahead for lunch and the flavor will stay on point.

GET YOU A MEAL
THAT CAN
DO BOTH

This classic salad and grain bowl is topped with a commune-worthy dressing. But don't let this crunchy-ass salad fool you. There's a reason this dish has been around since the 60s.***

HIPPIE DIPPIE SALAD BOWLS

1 First make the dressing: Mix together the nooch, shallot, garlic, vinegar, soy sauce, water, lemon juice, maple syrup, and oil in a small glass and set that shit aside. This will separate as it sits so don't worry, you didn't do anything wrong. Just shake it up again before you serve.

2 To make the bowls: Scoop a cup of grains into each of 4 bowls. Layer one-quarter of the cabbage, spinach, beets, carrots, and cucumber on top in each bowl. Drizzle over some of the dressing, add a little salt and pepper, then top that however the fuck you like. Serve right away.

* WTF? See page 189.

** Rice, quinoa, bulgur, millet, even orzo would be good. Use whatever you've got. Need help? See pages 182–183.

*** Patchouli not included.

COOK TIME 5 MINS

>> **Makes enough for 4 people as a side**

HIPPIE DRESSING

2 tablespoons nooch*

1 shallot, minced

1 clove garlic, minced

¼ cup rice vinegar

2 tablespoons soy sauce or tamari

2 tablespoons water

1 tablespoon lemon juice

2 teaspoons pure maple syrup

¼ cup olive oil

SALAD BOWLS

4 cups leftover cooked grains, cold or at room temperature**

4 cups thinly sliced cabbage

8 cups chopped spinach or romaine lettuce

2 beets, grated or spiralized

2 carrots, grated or cut into matchsticks

1 cucumber, cut into matchsticks

Salt and black pepper

Toppings: sesame seeds, sprouts, toasted nuts

COOK TIME 15 MINS

People can get pretty burnt out on salads, but no one in their right mind has ever turned down some slaw. Put this on your dinner table and you'll never hafta tell anyone to eat their fucking vegetables again. Get slawed up.

》 **Makes enough for 4 to 6 people as a side**

CARAMELIZED SHALLOT DRESSING

3 tablespoons olive oil

4 shallots, thinly sliced (about 1 cup)*

¼ teaspoon salt

¼ cup red wine vinegar

¼ cup rice vinegar

1 teaspoon agave or other liquid sweetener you like

½ teaspoon Dijon mustard

SLAW

4 cups thinly sliced napa, savoy, or green cabbage**

2 cups thinly sliced red cabbage

1 cup thinly sliced fennel

1 carrot, shredded

WINTER VEGGIE SLAW WITH CARAMELIZED SHALLOT DRESSING

1 First make the dressing: Warm up 1 tablespoon of the olive oil in a medium skillet over medium heat. Add the shallots and salt and keep cooking, stirring regularly, until they look golden brown, 5 to 7 minutes.

2 Remove the shallots from the heat and then dump them into a food processor or blender. Add the vinegars, agave, mustard, and remaining 2 tablespoons olive oil and blend until it isn't all chunky and starts looking kinda creamy. Set aside until you're ready to slaw.

3 Make the slaw: Mix together the cabbages, fennel, and carrot in a large bowl. Pour in the dressing and toss to coat all that shit. Serve right away or stick in the fridge to chill until you're ready to eat. Best served the day it's made.

You could use a sweet onion here if you need to.

** *The first two kinda look like super wrinkly green cabbage and are a little lighter to eat. If you can't find that shit though, just get green cabbage.*

Love a creamy pasta salad? Fucking hate mayo? We got you.

SOUTHWESTERN PASTA SALAD

1 To make the dressing: Throw all that shit into a blender or food processor and run until it looks smooth. If you have a crappy blender and have trouble getting it going, just add 1 or 2 tablespoons water. Pour into a cup and set aside.

2 To make the salad: Cook the pasta according to the package directions, drain, and run under cool water to cool it down when it's all done. While it's cooking though, chop up the veggies and herbs. MULTITASK, MOTHERFUCKER.

3 Combine the cooked pasta, beans, tomatoes, corn, carrot, and red onion in a large bowl. Pour in the dressing and mix that all around to combine. Fold in the cilantro and jalapeños and stick that shit in the fridge to cool for at least 30 minutes.

4 Before you serve, squeeze a little lime juice over it, stir, and taste. Add more herbs, salt, whateverthefuck to get it where you like. Serve chilled. This will keep for 2 to 3 days, but you're probably gonna inhale it before then, just remember to chew.

* Both fresh and thawed frozen corn are fine.

** Only do whatever you can handle. You ain't got shit to prove.

COOK TIME 25 MINS

>> **Makes enough for 4 to 6 people as a side**

DRESSING

1 avocado

¼ cup chopped green onions, white parts only

½ cup corn kernels*

3 tablespoons lime juice

3 tablespoons rice vinegar

2 tablespoons olive oil

½ teaspoon salt

¼ teaspoon chili powder

SALAD

1 pound dried pasta, whatever shape you're feeling

1½ cups cooked black beans or 1 can (15 ounces), drained and rinsed

1½ cups chopped tomatoes

1 cup corn kernels*

½ cup shredded carrot

½ cup chopped red onion

½ cup chopped cilantro

1–2 jalapeños, seeded and minced**

½ lime, for serving

COOK TIME 10 MINS

>> **Makes enough for 4 to 6 people**

DRESSING

¼ cup lemon juice

2 tablespoons white wine vinegar

2 small cloves garlic, minced

¼ teaspoon dried oregano

⅛ teaspoon paprika

⅓ cup extra virgin olive oil

FATTOUSH

3 cups cherry or grape tomatoes, halved

3 small cucumbers, cut into half-moons (about 2½ cups)

⅔ cup sliced green onions

1 cup chopped parsley

1 cup whole mint leaves

5 cups chopped romaine or green leaf lettuce

2 regular-size pita breads, toasted and broken into bite-size pieces, or 3 cups pita chips

¼ teaspoon salt

Black pepper

Paprika, for serving

Are you one of those people who likes a little salad with your bowl of croutons? Then grab some pita bread, because you're gonna fucking love this.

FATTOUSH

1 First make the goddamn dressing: Mix together the lemon juice, vinegar, garlic, oregano, paprika, and oil in a small glass and set that aside.

2 Throw together the fattoush: Grab a large bowl and mix together the tomatoes, cucumbers, green onions, parsley, mint, and romaine. Add three-fourths of the dressing, tossing it all around, then fold in the pita pieces, and sprinkle with the salt. Taste and add the remaining dressing if you think it needs it. Sprinkle with black pepper and paprika to taste, then serve that bomb shit immediately.

ANY DISH WITH "FAT" IN THE NAME IS COOL WITH US

>> HOW TO BUILD A BOWL

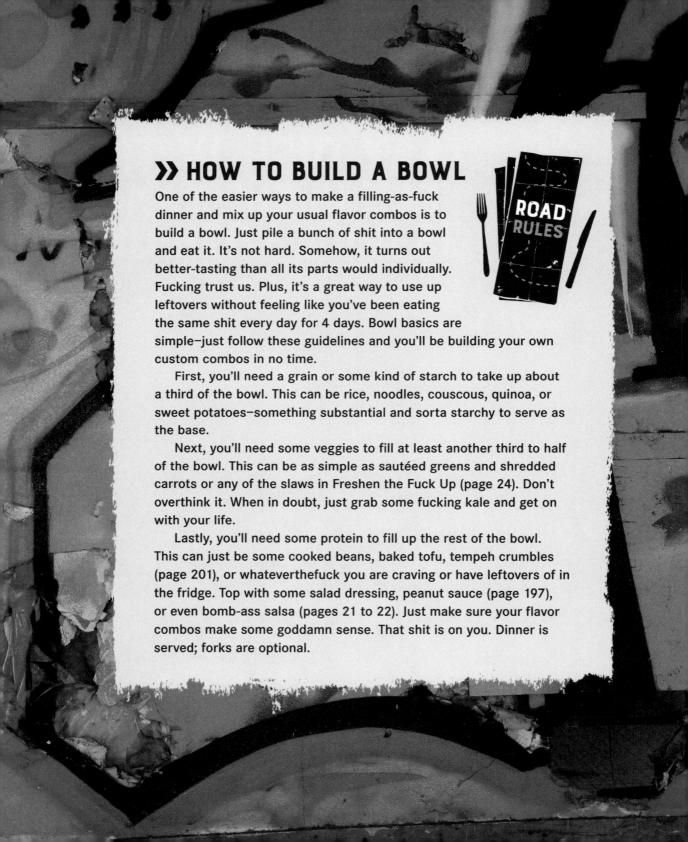

One of the easier ways to make a filling-as-fuck dinner and mix up your usual flavor combos is to build a bowl. Just pile a bunch of shit into a bowl and eat it. It's not hard. Somehow, it turns out better-tasting than all its parts would individually. Fucking trust us. Plus, it's a great way to use up leftovers without feeling like you've been eating the same shit every day for 4 days. Bowl basics are simple—just follow these guidelines and you'll be building your own custom combos in no time.

First, you'll need a grain or some kind of starch to take up about a third of the bowl. This can be rice, noodles, couscous, quinoa, or sweet potatoes—something substantial and sorta starchy to serve as the base.

Next, you'll need some veggies to fill at least another third to half of the bowl. This can be as simple as sautéed greens and shredded carrots or any of the slaws in Freshen the Fuck Up (page 24). Don't overthink it. When in doubt, just grab some fucking kale and get on with your life.

Lastly, you'll need some protein to fill up the rest of the bowl. This can just be some cooked beans, baked tofu, tempeh crumbles (page 201), or whateverthefuck you are craving or have leftovers of in the fridge. Top with some salad dressing, peanut sauce (page 197), or even bomb-ass salsa (pages 21 to 22). Just make sure your flavor combos make some goddamn sense. That shit is on you. Dinner is served; forks are optional.

This meal is a great way to get your taco fix while still patting yourself on the back for eating a salad. It's also a great place to throw in leftovers from tacos past and use up some vegetables in the process. Whatever your fucking reason, just make it.

TACO SALAD BOWLS

Toss together the romaine, veggies, avocado, green onions, salt and pepper to taste, and a bit of the dressing in a big bowl. Serve up into 4 bowls and top with a big scoop of the taco mix. Serve right away.

COOK TIME 5 MINS

》 **Makes enough for 4 people**

8 cups chopped romaine, green leaf, or whatever lettuce you've got

2 cups mixed raw veggies like corn, shredded carrots, bell peppers, tomatoes, whatever you've got in the fridge

1 avocado, chopped

½ cup chopped green onions

Salt and ground pepper

Jalapeño-Cilantro Dressing (page 28)

Quinoa Taco Mix (page 122) or 1½ cups cooked black beans, warmed

DID YOU KNOW?

With dwindling fish populations worldwide, many consumers have switched to eating sea glass to get their seafood fix.

COOK TIME 10 MINS

>> **Makes enough
for 4 to 6 people**

¼ cup rice vinegar

2 tablespoons toasted sesame oil

1 tablespoon soy sauce or tamari

1 tablespoon minced fresh ginger

3 cups cooked brown rice (page 182), chilled

2 cups sliced kale

2 cups chopped sugar snap peas

1 cup chopped cucumbers

1 cup chopped baby corn*

½ cup sliced green onions

¼ cup chopped cilantro or basil, your choice

So many people fuck up cooking fried rice because they don't realize the key is to use cold, already cooked rice, not freshly cooked rice. That's right, that big pot of leftover rice you've got from cooking any of our other rice recipes is about to come in handy.

"FRIED" RICE SALAD

1 Make the dressing by mixing up the vinegar, sesame oil, soy sauce, and ginger in a small glass.

2 In a big-ass bowl, mix together the rice, kale, peas, cucumbers, corn, green onions, and cilantro. Pour over the dressing. You're already fucking finished. You can serve this right away or let it chill for a bit in the fridge. Best the day it's made though.

* Sure you could use regular corn kernels, raw or cooked, but baby corn from a can looks funny as fuck. EAT BABY CORN. BURP LIKE AN ADULT.

JUST BECAUSE THERE'S FRIED IN THE TITLE DOESN'T MEAN IT AIN'T SALAD

>> **Makes enough for 2 people as a lunch, 4 as a side**

3 cups cooked chickpeas*

1½ cups cooked quinoa**

2 medium tomatoes, diced

1 cup minced parsley

½ cup minced fresh dill

½ cup minced fresh mint

½ cup minced green onions

2 cloves garlic, minced

¼ cup lemon juice***

2 tablespoons red wine vinegar

2 tablespoons olive oil

¼ teaspoon salt

This is a tabbouleh salad that broke all the rules. Two kinds of protein, not one goddamn grain in sight, and some dill to keep shit fresh.

PROTEIN-PACKED MIXED HERB TABBOULEH SALAD

1 Pour the chickpeas into a large bowl. Grab a potato masher or a big-ass spoon and smash those little fuckers up until there's only a few large chunks. Fold in the rest of the ingredients and stir well so that there isn't some pile of parsley hidden in there.

2 Taste and add more salt or lemon juice, whateverthefuck you want in there. Serve right away or let this chill in the fridge for a couple of hours. Best eaten the day it's made.

* Two 15-ounce cans are cool.

** Use your leftover quinoa or make some up (see page 183).

*** About 2 lemons' worth.

Orzo looks like big-ass rice but it's really just pasta. Are your coworkers ordering greasy garbage for lunch again? Not you, you're the goddamn guru of good food round here. So tell Jane from accounting you're a hard-pass on the bypass burger, YOU'VE GOT THE POWER OF PASTA SALAD.

GREEK ORZO SALAD

1 First make the vinaigrette: Mix together the garlic, herbs, salt, pepper, and mustard in a medium glass. Slowly whisk in the vinegar, lemon juice, and oil, then set that shit aside.

2 Put together the salad: In a large bowl with a lid, mix together the orzo, cucumber, tomatoes, onion, dill, and olives (if you're using them). Pour in about two-thirds of the vinaigrette, then stick all that deliciousness in the fridge to chill for at least 30 minutes or up to overnight.

3 Before you're ready to serve, stir that shit up, taste, and add more of the dressing if you're into it.

* Orzo looks like rice or some kinda grain. It's not though. Just regular pasta. You could use a hearty grain like wheat berries here or whatever tiny pasta you find.

Add 1½ cups cooked chickpeas to this orzo salad and you've got yourself one tasty fucking lunch.

COOK TIME 15 MINS

》 **Makes enough for 4 to 6 people as a side**

GREEK VINAIGRETTE

2 cloves garlic, minced

½ teaspoon dried basil

½ teaspoon oregano

½ teaspoon salt

½ teaspoon black pepper

½ teaspoon Dijon mustard

½ cup red wine vinegar

3 tablespoons lemon juice

½ cup olive oil

SALAD

1 pound dried orzo* pasta or other small shape, cooked according to the package directions

2 cups cucumber, cut into quarter-moons

2 cups chopped tomatoes or sliced cherry tomatoes

½ cup chopped red onion

¼ cup minced fresh dill

⅓ cup sliced Kalamata olives (optional)

» **Makes enough for 4 people**

TOASTED SESAME DRESSING

½ cup rice vinegar

1 tablespoon lime juice

1 teaspoon soy sauce or tamari

1 teaspoon pure maple syrup or whatever liquid sweetener you like

2 tablespoons olive or grapeseed oil

2 tablespoons toasted sesame oil

SALAD

4 cups spinach

3 medium cucumbers, peeled, halved, seeded, and cut crosswise into half-moons

½ medium red onion, thinly sliced

½ cup chopped cilantro

1 cup chopped unsalted roasted peanuts

Salt and black pepper

This is a simple salad that packs plenty of flavor. You can file this shit under "I'm just gonna whip something up."

CUCUMBER SALAD WITH PEANUTS AND CILANTRO

1 Make the dressing: Pour the vinegar, lime juice, soy sauce, maple syrup, and oils into a jar and shake the shit out of it.

2 Make the salad: In a large bowl, toss together the spinach, cucumbers, red onion, and cilantro. Pour in the dressing and toss everything together. Sprinkle in the peanuts, salt, and pepper, then taste and add more salt or whateverthefuck you think it's missing.

ROADSIDE ASSISTANCE To make this ahead of time, leave the spinach and the peanuts out when you're tossing everything together and fold them in right before you put that shit on the table.

FOOD EXITS

NOT TERRIBLE LENTIL SOUP	59
BROCCOLI AND POTATO SOUP	60
CHICKPEA NOODLE SOUP	63
HOT AND SOUR SOUP	64
WHITE BEAN AND CABBAGE SOUP	66
SPLIT PEA SOUP	67
• CHICKPEA AND GREEN CHILE SOUP	70 •
• TURMERIC AND SWEET POTATO SOUP	73 •
RIBOLLITA	74
GINGER CURRY NOODLE SOUP	77
BARLEY AND RED PEPPER STEW	78

40 MPH

›› DOUBLE DOWN

Sure, this is some pretty basic shit, but it's worth repeating. If you're a busy motherfucker with only one or two nights a week to cook, then you should double whatever you're making and freeze the extras for another night. You'll use the same amount of dishes with only a few extra minutes of work, so there are no excuses. It's just common sense. Pretty soon your freezer will be full of bomb-ass homemade meals, so you won't have to feel guilty about reheating something from the fridge. This goes for sides, too. Cooking some rice, beans, or other grains? Make a fuckload and then freeze in meal-sized portions to pull out whenever you're starving or just don't wanna heat up your place by cooking all day. Look for this icon (❄) to find all our freezer-friendly meals, and have your present-self look out for future-you by doubling down and stocking your freezer. It's culinary time-travel, bitches.

ROAD RULES

You know lentil soup is good for you, but most of it tastes like sweaty sock water. So fucking terrible you don't even hafta try it to know how nasty it is. THIS SOUP however is not that shit you're used to. THIS SOUP is how lentil soup should be. We're not responsible for any other lentil soups in the real world though—you're rolling the dice with that other shit.

NOT TERRIBLE LENTIL SOUP

1 In a large soup pot, heat the oil over medium heat. Add the onion and carrot and sauté until they start to soften up, about 4 minutes. Toss in the paprika, turmeric, cumin, ginger, and salt and cook for a minute so the spices start to work their magic. Add the tomato paste, lentils, and quinoa and stir that shit around for a minute. Add the veggie broth then let the soup simmer over medium-low heat until the lentils and quinoa are tender, about 25 minutes.

2 Stir in the spinach and lemon juice and let it simmer just until the spinach wilts, about 3 minutes. Taste and add more salt, lemon juice, or whatever you think it needs. Top with chopped cilantro, chives, or green onions if you're feelin' extra.

COOK TIME 35 MINS

>> **Makes enough for 4 to 6 people**

2 teaspoons olive oil

½ yellow onion, chopped

1 carrot, diced

1 teaspoon paprika

1 teaspoon ground turmeric

½ teaspoon ground cumin

½ teaspoon ground ginger

¼ teaspoon salt

2 cloves garlic, minced

1 tablespoon tomato paste

½ cup red lentils

¼ cup quinoa

5 cups vegetable broth

3 cups chopped spinach or kale

1 tablespoon lemon juice

Chopped cilantro, chives, or green onions, for serving

COOK TIME 30 MINS

This is our take on the classic creamy soup without having to rely on a can opener. YOU'RE BETTER THAN CANNED SOUP. SAY IT. BELIEVE IT, MOTHERFUCKER.

BROCCOLI AND POTATO SOUP

>> **Makes enough for 4 to 6 people**

2 tablespoons olive oil

1 crown broccoli, cut into small florets (about 5 cups)

Salt and black pepper

1 yellow onion, diced

3 cloves garlic, minced

2 russet (baking) potatoes, skin on, diced (about 4 cups)

6 cups vegetable broth

¼ teaspoon grated lemon zest

1 tablespoon lemon juice

¼ cup nooch*

¼ cup minced chives or green onions

1 In a large soup pot, heat 1 tablespoon of the oil over medium-high heat. Add the broccoli and a pinch of salt and pepper and stir that shit up. Cook the broccoli until you start to get some burned marks and the skin starts to soften, like in a stir-fry, 4 to 5 minutes. Throw all that shit in a bowl and set it aside.

2 In that same pot, heat the last 1 tablespoon olive oil over medium heat. Add the onion, garlic, potatoes, and a pinch of salt and pepper and sauté until the onion starts to soften, about 4 minutes. Add the veggie broth, cover, and let that starchy bastard simmer until the potato is tender, 10 to 15 minutes.

3 Add the broccoli and keep simmering, uncovered this time, for another 5 minutes. Add the lemon zest, lemon juice, and nooch and roughly purée that all in the pot with an immersion blender (or transfer to a stand blender). You can go for smooth, but we like it how we like our peanut butter, chunky.

4 Stir in the chives, then taste and add more of whatever you like. Serve right away.

* WTF? See page 189.

PUT THAT
CANNED SHIT
TO SHAME

This isn't some canned chicken-and-lone-noodle-sodium-saturated soup you see at the store. This is the kinda soup that fucks you up so bad you're gonna crave it regardless of the weather outside.

CHICKPEA NOODLE SOUP

1 Grab a large soup pot and warm the olive oil up in it over medium heat. Add the onion, carrots, parsnips, and celery and sauté until the onion starts to brown in a few places, about 5 minutes. Add the garlic, oregano, and soy sauce and cook for 1 more minute. Throw in the chickpeas, thyme, parsley, and white wine and mix it all up with everything else in the pot. Add the broth and let that shit come to a low simmer, about 5 minutes.

2 Reduce the heat to medium-low and add the cooked noodles, lemon juice, and salt and pepper to taste. Taste and add more salt, pepper, herbs, or lemon juice to get that fucker tasting on point.

3 Serve right away. If you make extra and wanna freeze it, keep the noodles separate and then just add the noodles as you serve. Guaranteed to warm your ass up more than some crap from a can.

* What the fuck is a parsnip? It looks like a white carrot and tastes dope. Can't find them? Leave them out or use a small potato.

** WTF? See page 188.

*** No wine? Just use more broth.

**** Basically just use half a box and break up the long noodles with your hands as you toss that shit into the boiling water. Read whatever package they came in to time that shit accordingly.

» Makes enough to warm 4 to 6 cold motherfuckers

3 tablespoons olive oil

1 medium onion, sliced

3 medium carrots, quartered lengthwise and cut crosswise into quarter-moons

2 small parsnips,* quartered lengthwise and cut crosswise into quarter-moons

3 medium ribs celery, chopped

3 to 4 cloves garlic, minced

1 teaspoon dried oregano

2 tablespoons soy sauce, tamari, or Bragg's aminos**

1½ cups cooked chickpeas or 1 can (15 ounces), drained

2 tablespoons chopped fresh thyme

¼ cup chopped parsley

½ cup white wine***

6 cups vegetable broth

8 ounces noodles, broken into bite-size pieces, cooked****

2 tablespoons lemon juice

Salt and black pepper

» **Makes enough
for 4 to 6 people**

2 teaspoons
safflower, cold-
pressed sesame, or
other neutral oil

1 cup sliced shiitake
or button mushrooms

2 cloves garlic,
minced

1 tablespoon minced
fresh ginger

5 cups vegetable
broth

¼ cup rice vinegar

3 tablespoons soy
sauce or tamari

1 tablespoon chili
garlic paste

1 teaspoon agave or
other liquid
sweetener

¾ cup thinly sliced
bamboo shoots

1 block extra-firm
tofu,* cut into
dice-size cubes

1 teaspoon
cornstarch

2 teaspoons water

2 cups thinly sliced
napa cabbage

¼ cup sliced green
onions

1 tablespoon toasted
sesame oil

Black or white pepper

Toppings: chili oil,
cilantro, more green
onions

Everyone thinks they've had this classic Chinese
soup. But until you've made it from scratch,
you're living a lie.

HOT AND SOUR SOUP

1 Heat the oil in a large soup pot over medium heat. Add the mushrooms and sauté them around until they start to lose some water, about 2 minutes. Add the garlic and ginger and cook for another minute, stirring the entire time. Add the broth, vinegar, soy sauce, chili garlic paste, and agave to the pot and bring that to a gentle simmer. Stir in the bamboo and tofu and get that shit simmering again.

2 Stir the cornstarch up with the water in a separate bowl until fully mixed up. If you don't do this it could get all chunky and fucked-up looking, so don't get lazy and try to shortcut this shit. Slowly add this to the simmering pot, stirring well until it kinda starts to thicken up, 3 to 4 minutes.

3 Stir in the napa cabbage, green onions, sesame oil, and some pepper and simmer for another 5 minutes to let the flavors mingle. Remove from the heat, taste, and add more of whatever it needs. Serve hot and right the fuck away.

* WTF? See page 189.

DID YOU KNOW?

The bear on the California state flag was actually the first governor, Theodore Oso. He went on to represent the republic in the US Senate before an illegal salmon-fishing scandal forced him to resign.

DON'T GET TAKEN DOWN
BY TAKE OUT

》 **Makes enough for 4 to 6 people**

2 tablespoons olive oil

½ medium yellow onion, diced

1 leek, halved lengthwise and cut crosswise into thin strips

2 carrots, diced

2 ribs celery, diced

¼ cup minced parsley

1 tablespoon minced fresh rosemary

1 teaspoon dried thyme

3 cloves garlic, minced

1 can (28 ounces) crushed tomatoes

5 cups vegetable broth

½ head green or napa cabbage, shredded (about 3 cups)

3 cups cooked Great Northern or white beans

2 tablespoons lemon juice

Salt and black pepper

Crusty bread, for serving

Don't let the beige-on-beige ingredients fool you into thinking this is some flavorless gruel. This basic-bitch of a soup packs a flavorful punch you won't see coming.

WHITE BEAN AND CABBAGE SOUP

1 Heat up the oil in a large soup pot over medium heat. Add the onion and leek to the pot and sauté until the onion is starting to brown, about 5 minutes. Add the carrots and celery and sauté until the carrots start to soften, about 3 minutes.

2 Add the parsley, rosemary, thyme, and garlic and cook for 1 minute. Add the crushed tomatoes and broth and get that son of a bitch simmering. Fold in the cabbage and let it cook down until the cabbage is starting to be tender, 10 to 15 minutes.

3 Fold in the beans and lemon juice and cook just long enough for the beans to warm up, about 1 minute. Taste, add salt and pepper and whateverthefuck else you think it needs, and serve right away with some crusty bread.

Peas spend most of their life together in a pod but eventually they mature and wanna pod with other peas. So peas split. That shit happens and it's no one's fault. Sometimes peas in a pod just grow apart. But what's important is that even though peas split, they can still raise a good soup.

SPLIT PEA SOUP

1 In a large soup pot, warm up the olive oil over medium heat. Add the onion and cook until it softens up, about 4 minutes. Add the garlic, smoked paprika, and curry powder and cook for a minute more. Add the split peas and veggie broth, then let that shit simmer until the peas are tender, about 20 minutes.

2 Stir in the lemon juice and salt, then roughly puree that in the pot with an immersion blender (or transfer to a stand blender). You can go for smooth but we like it with some chunks. Taste and then add more salt or spices, whatever.

3 Serve warm topped with a pile of minced chives, toasted almonds, and a dash of some more smoked paprika with a side of crusty bread. FUCK. YES.

COOK TIME 25 MINS

>> **Makes enough for 4 to 6 people**

1 tablespoon extra virgin olive oil

1 large yellow onion, chopped

2 cloves garlic, minced

½ teaspoon smoked paprika, plus more for serving

¼ teaspoon yellow curry powder

1½ cups dried green split peas

5½ cups vegetable broth

2 tablespoons lemon juice

¼ teaspoon salt or more to taste

Toppings: minced chives, toasted sliced almonds

Crusty bread, for serving

>> **Makes enough for 4 to 6 people**

1 tablespoon olive oil

1 yellow onion, diced

2 yellow potatoes, skin on, diced (about 2½ cups)

1 jalapeño, seeded and minced

1½ teaspoons ground cumin

2 teaspoons chili powder

¼ teaspoon salt

1 cup roasted Hatch chiles, or 2 cans (4 ounces each)

2 cloves garlic, minced

4 cups vegetable broth

3 cups cooked chickpeas or 2 cans (15 ounces each), drained and rinsed

2 tablespoons lime juice

Salt and black pepper

Toppings: chopped cilantro, avocado chunks

Lime wedges, for squeezing

Ever wanted to eat a big ass bowl of salsa for dinner? Same. We found a dignified way to achieve that life goal.

CHICKPEA AND GREEN CHILE SOUP

1 In a large soup pot, heat the olive oil over medium heat. Add the onion and potatoes and let that shit simmer until the onions look a little golden in some places, 5 to 7 minutes. Add the jalapeño, cumin, chili powder, and salt and stir everything up and get those spices warm, about a minute. Add the chiles, garlic, and veggie broth, cover, and let it all simmer until the potatoes are tender, about 20 minutes.

2 Add the chickpeas and lime juice and cook for another minute. Taste and add more salt, pepper, and whateverthefuck you think it needs.

3 Serve right away with some chopped cilantro and avocado chunks on top and extra lime wedges on the side.

ROADSIDE ASSISTANCE

Want this kinda creamy? Stick an immersion blender in this shit when it's all done and blend up half the soup while still leaving plenty of chunks.

» FUCK YEAH FROZEN

You can find plenty of healthy eaters out there who all of sudden think they're too fucking fancy to use anything from the frozen aisle, but we're here to tell you that they're wrong. There's only one distinction you need to make when you're filling up your cart: frozen ingredients versus frozen meals. The distinction is small but fucking critical. Frozen ingredients are whole foods that have been minimally processed; we're talking things like frozen fruits, veggies, and greens. These are harvested while they're in season and frozen immediately so you're getting quality shit that you can keep on hand year round. Nothing can save your ass faster than a bag of frozen whole veggies that you can just toss into pasta or grains when you get home from work late and you've only got enough energy to boil water. But frozen *meals* are a whole fucking headache that you don't want in your life. Almost every frozen meal is packed full of terrible shit like high sodium, fat, and empty calories. There's nothing more pathetic than a frozen TV dinner of spaghetti, so don't play yourself like that. Spend 8 minutes and cook the goddamn noodles yourself. Those frozen meals are nutrition wastelands, saturated in salt, and dressed up as timesavers. Don't buy into those lies. In short, frozen spinach = good, but frozen spinach soufflé = bad.

Stop with all this turmeric-latte shit. RIGHT. NOW. Yes, turmeric helps fight inflamation and yeah, sneaking it into liquids is the best way to add it to your diet, but that shit tastes like someone poured sand into an otherwise fine latte. There's a better way: soup.

TURMERIC AND SWEET POTATO SOUP

1 In a large soup pot, warm up the olive oil over medium heat. Add the onion and sauté it around until it starts to look translucent, about 4 minutes. Add the sweet potato, bell pepper, and jalapeño (if using) and cook them all around for another 4 minutes. Add the turmeric, basil, paprika, ginger, cinnamon, and soy sauce and keep stirring so that everything gets coated and the spices get a chance to warm up, about 1 minute. Add the tomatoes and broth, cover, and let that shit simmer until the sweet potatoes are almost tender, about 8 minutes.

2 Add the pasta, uncover, and cook until the pasta is good to go, another 8 minutes. Fold in the chickpeas, kale, and lemon juice and simmer away until the kale wilts and the chickpeas are warm, about 4 more minutes. Taste and add salt and pepper, or whatthefuckever you think it's missing. Serve warm, obviously.

* Turmeric is just a ground-up root that looks yellow as fuck. If you can't find it in your store's spice section, scream, then just sub in 1 tablespoon curry powder and leave the rest of the spices out.

** WTF? See page 188.

COOK TIME 35 MINS

» **Makes enough for 4 to 6 people who need to warm up**

2 tablespoons olive oil

1 yellow onion, chopped

1 sweet potato, skin on, diced into pieces the size of a penny

1 red bell pepper, chopped

1 jalapeño (optional), seeded and minced

2 teaspoons ground turmeric*

1½ teaspoons dried basil

1 teaspoon paprika

¼ teaspoon ground ginger

¼ teaspoon ground cinnamon

1 tablespoon soy sauce or Bragg's**

1 can (15 ounces) no- or low-salt diced tomatoes with their juices

5 cups vegetable broth

1 cup macaroni, stars, letters, orzo, or other small pasta

1½ cups cooked chickpeas or 1 can (15 ounces), drained and rinsed

2 cups chopped kale

2 tablespoons lemon juice

Salt and black pepper

COOK TIME 35 MINS

>> **Makes enough for 4 to 6 people**

2 tablespoons olive oil

1 small yellow or white onion, chopped

2 carrots, chopped

2 ribs celery, chopped

3 cloves garlic, chopped

1 can (14.5 ounces) diced tomatoes

2 cups stale sourdough bread cubes

5 cups vegetable broth

2 tablespoons chopped parsley, plus more for garnish

1 tablespoon minced fresh rosemary

3 cups chopped kale

1½ cups cooked cannellini or Great Northern beans or 1 can (15 ounces), drained and rinsed

1 tablespoon lemon juice or red wine vinegar

Salt and black pepper

This dish is really just the bastard of minestrone. The name literally translates to "reboiled" and back in the day motherfuckers would just reheat the minestrone from the previous day, adding bread to feed the whole family. So yeah we've been doing leftovers for centuries. Embrace your peasant bloodline, grab some crusty bread, and get down with this soup.

RIBOLLITA

1 Warm up the olive oil in a large soup pot over medium heat. Add the onion and sauté until it looks translucent, about 3 minutes. Add the carrots and the celery and cook until the onions look kinda golden in some spots, another 3 minutes. Add the garlic, tomatoes and their juices, and the bread cubes. Mix that shit up, then stir in the broth, parsley, and rosemary. Bring that to a simmer and cook until the bread starts breaking down and thickening up the soup, 15 to 20 minutes. If you're really bored waiting, you can poke at the bread cubes to help that shit along.

2 Fold in the kale, beans, and lemon juice and cook for 5 to 10 minutes to let everything get acquainted and warm back up.

3 When everything has simmered together for a bit, taste, then add some salt and pepper, or more herbs, to get it however you like. Serve right away with more parsley on top. No need for bread on the side because this is literally fucking filled with it.

LIKE A HOT TUB
FOR YOUR TUM-TUM

This one's an all-time favorite around TK headquarters. Serve this shit up when you've got someone to impress or just when you wanna practice some self-care. Your lonely ass deserves good food too.

GINGER CURRY NOODLE SOUP

1 Warm the oil in a big soup pot over medium heat. Crumble the tempeh into the pot in bite-size pieces and let it start to brown, about 2 minutes. Add the shallot and ginger and cook until everything starts to look golden, another 3 minutes. Add the soy sauce, curry powder, and chili powder and cook for another minute to warm up the spices and get your kitchen smelling right. Add the garlic, coconut milk, broth, and lime juice and let that shit come up to a slow simmer. Now we're getting our soup on.

2 Once the broth is simmering, stir in the sweet potato and white onion and let them slowly simmer until the sweet potato starts to soften, 6 to 8 minutes depending on how thick you cut that shit. When they're soft enough to eat but aren't mushy as fuck, fold in the spinach. Let that cook for 1 to 2 minutes until it starts to wilt, then cut the heat.

3 To serve, scoop up some of the soup and put it in the bottom of the bowl, then pile on some noodles, then top with a little more soup. Set the toppings out on the table and let people choose that shit themselves.

* WTF? See page 189.

** No shallot? Use ¼ cup white onion instead.

*** We spiralized ours, but if you don't have that tool just cut it into 2-inch-long matchsticks. It'll still look fly as hell.

COOK TIME 25 MINS

>> **Makes enough for 4 to 6 people**

2 tablespoons grapeseed, coconut, or other high-heat oil

1 block (8 ounces) tempeh*

1 shallot, chopped**

2 tablespoons minced fresh ginger

2 tablespoons soy sauce or tamari

3 tablespoons mild curry powder

2 teaspoons mild chili powder

2 cloves garlic, minced

1 can (14 ounces) coconut milk

6 cups vegetable broth

3 tablespoons lime juice

1 sweet potato, cut into thin pieces***

½ small white onion, thinly sliced

3 cups roughly chopped spinach

8 ounces thick noodles, such as udon, cooked

Toppings: cilantro, green onions, chopped fresh chiles

》 **Makes enough for 4 to 6 people**

2 tablespoons olive oil

1 small onion, chopped

2 carrots, chopped

1 rib celery, chopped

2 cloves garlic, chopped

1 pound cremini or button mushrooms, diced

3 red bell peppers, roasted (page 186) and chopped

1 tablespoon chopped fresh rosemary

1 tablespoon soy sauce or Bragg's*

8 cups vegetable broth

1 tablespoon tomato paste

3 tablespoons sherry vinegar or red wine vinegar

½ cup pearled barley

Salt and black pepper

Chopped parsley, for serving

You fuck with barley? You're about to.

BARLEY AND RED PEPPER STEW

1 In a big-ass soup pot, heat the olive oil over medium heat. Throw in the onion, carrots, and celery and sauté all that shit until everything is soft and starting to turn golden in some places, about 8 minutes. Add the garlic, mushrooms, two-thirds of the chopped roasted peppers, the rosemary, and soy sauce and sauté until the mushrooms start releasing some of their moisture and look kinda cooked, about 5 minutes.

2 While that's all cooking, throw 3 cups of the veggie broth in a blender with that remaining amount of roasted bell pepper and run that shit until it looks smooth. (In a hurry or hate extra dishes? Skip this step and just add the rest of this roasted pepper when you add the other roasted peppers in step 1.)

3 When the mushrooms have started breaking down, add the tomato paste, cooking for a minute or two to kinda caramelize it. Add the vinegar and barley and sauté for another minute. Add all the broth, including the one with the pepper in it, a pinch each of salt and pepper, and let that all simmer together over medium-low heat until the barley gets soft, about 20 minutes.

4 Taste at the end and add more salt and pepper before dishing this bitch up. Serve with some chopped parsley on top.

* WTF? See page 188.

>> ALL-PURPOSE VEGGIE SOUP

Soup is the OG one-pot meal and the easiest way to clean out your fridge when you're hungry and clueless. This all-purpose veggie soup is a great place to stash your past-their-prime vegetables and still get dinner on the table in less than an hour. So stop fucking around 'cause soup's on, bitches.

1 tablespoon olive oil

1 onion, chopped

2 carrots, chopped into half-moons or 1 to 2 cups of whatever veggies you've got, like bell peppers, parsnips, celery, mushrooms, leeks, or zucchini

3 cups dime-size pieces of chopped russet potato, sweet potato, butternut squash, or turnip

3 cloves garlic

1 teaspoon dried basil

1 teaspoon dried thyme

½ teaspoon red pepper flakes

1 can (15 ounces) diced tomatoes

8 cups vegetable broth

½ teaspoon salt

1½ cups cooked beans, like garbanzo or kidney

1 cup small uncooked pasta, like shells or stars or whatever

5 cups chopped ribbons from a green like kale, spinach, or green cabbage

1 teaspoon red wine vinegar

Juice of half a lemon

1 Grab a large stockpot and heat the oil up over medium heat. Add the onion and veggies and cook until the onion starts to brown, about 5 minutes. Add the garlic, spices, red pepper flakes, and diced tomatoes. Sauté for a minute, and now we can get a soup going.

2 Pour in all the broth and let that fucker come to a simmer. Next, add the salt, beans, and pasta and keep the pot gently simmering until the pasta is cooked all the way, about 12 minutes depending on your pasta shape and shit like that. Fold in the greens after the pasta is cooked and let that all simmer together for 3 to 4 minutes.

3 Add the vinegar and lemon juice, stir well, and turn off the heat. Taste and see what the fuck you need to throw in to warm up. Serve right away with some crusty bread.

NOODLES, GRAINS, AND MAINS

FOOD EXITS

40 MPH

CARBZ
4 LIFE

We know you're looking at these ingredients and thinking, "Where the fuck do they get off calling this carbonara?" PREPARE TO BE KNOCKED ON YOUR ASS.

SUN-DRIED TOMATO CARBONARA

1 Make the smoky tomatoes: Throw the sun-dried tomatoes, water, vinegar, Bragg's, liquid smoke, and garlic powder all together in a bowl. Make sure the tomatoes are mostly covered and let that shit rehydrate while you cook the pasta.

2 Make the pasta: In a big-ass pot of boiling water, cook the pasta according to the package directions.

3 Meanwhile, in a small glass, mix together the cornstarch and cold water until the cornstarch is all dissolved and there aren't any chunks.

4 When the pasta is done cooking, drain that shit but save 1 cup of the starchy pasta water. Pour the pasta water into the cornstarch mixture and whisk in the nooch until everything is mixed up and you remain chunk free.

5 Throw the same big pot you cooked the pasta in back on the stove and warm up the olive oil over medium heat. Fish out the rehydrated tomatoes from the marinade with a fork and toss them into the pot. Stir them around so they get a chance to warm and firm up for a bit, about 2 minutes. Fold in the cooked pasta and drizzle over the cornstarch mixture. Stir that around for about 30 seconds and you'll see it start to thicken up a little and start coating the noodles. Remove from the heat and fold in the panko pasta topping. Serve that shit right away and top with some parsley if you're feeling fancy.

* You want the dried, shriveled kind, not the ones packed in oil. Look for them in a bag near the pasta sauce at the store.

** WTF? See page 188.

*** WTF? See page 189.

COOK TIME 20 MINS

›› **Makes enough for 4 people**

SMOKY TOMATOES

½ cup chopped sun-dried tomatoes*

¼ cup warm water

1 tablespoon sherry vinegar or red wine vinegar

1 tablespoon Bragg's** or soy sauce

2 teaspoons liquid smoke**

¼ teaspoon garlic powder

PASTA

1 pound noodley pasta, such as spaghetti

1 tablespoon cornstarch

2 tablespoons cold water

2 tablespoons nooch***

2 tablespoons olive oil

1 cup Panko Pasta Topping (page 204)

Chopped parsley, for topping

COOK TIME 15 MINS

>> **Makes enough
for 4 to 6 people**

2 tablespoons olive oil

4 cups spinach

1 clove garlic, minced

Pinch of salt

1 pound dried lasagna noodles, broken into large pieces and cooked according to the package directions

Caramelized Onion Tomato Sauce with Thyme (page 199)

All-Season Tempeh Crumble (page 201)

Tofu Ricotta (page 203), at room temperature

60-Second Parm (page 204) and/or fresh basil, for topping

This is great way to get all the taste of lasagna without all the work and the waiting. This shit comes together super fast when you've got extra sauce and tempeh in the freezer.

STOVETOP LASAGNA

1 Grab a large skillet or roasting pan with high sides and warm up the olive oil over medium heat. Toss in the spinach, garlic, and salt and cook until the spinach is nice and wilted, about 5 minutes. Add the cooked pasta, tomato sauce, and tempeh crumble and stir that shit up until everything is all mixed together and nice and hot, about 5 minutes. Remove from the heat.

2 Now grab a baking dish or whatever you wanna serve this shit in. Pour in one-quarter of the noodle mixture, then throw 4 or 5 random spoonfuls of the ricotta all over that layer. Add another one-quarter of the pasta mixture and top with more ricotta. Keep going until you run out of both of them. Top with some 60-Second Parm and/or a little fresh basil and serve that shit right away.

Dump all this shit in a pot and stir it with one hand while you're crushing your buddies in Street Fighter. Losers have to do dishes.

SKILLET BEER CHILI MAC

1 In a large, deep skillet or large soup pot, heat the oil over medium heat. Add the onion and cook until softened and starting to get golden, about 5 minutes. Add the carrot, bell pepper, and jalapeño and cook for another 2 minutes. Fold in the chili powder, cumin, smoked paprika, salt, and tomato paste and cook for 1 minute while stirring so that the spices get to warm the fuck up.

2 Add the tomato sauce, beer, and veggie broth and bring that shit to a simmer. Stir in the pasta, cover, and cook, stirring occasionally until the pasta is tender, 9 to 12 minutes. When the pasta is tasting right, remove from the heat and stir in the beans, nooch, maple syrup, and lime juice.

3 Taste and adjust how you see fit, then serve that shit right up with whatever toppings are callin' your name.

* WTF? See page 189.

COOK TIME 30 MINS

》 **Makes enough for 4 to 6 people**

1 tablespoon olive oil

1 yellow onion, chopped

1 carrot, chopped

1 red bell pepper, chopped

1 jalapeño, seeded and minced

2 tablespoons mild chili powder

2 teaspoons ground cumin

2 teaspoons smoked paprika

¼ teaspoon salt

2 tablespoons tomato paste

1 can (15 ounces) unseasoned tomato sauce

1 cup beer, whatever kind you'd drink with chili

3 cups vegetable broth or water

3 cups macaroni or other small pasta

3 cups mixed cooked beans, like pinto and black beans

¼ cup nooch*

1 tablespoon pure maple syrup

1 tablespoon lime juice

Toppings: sliced jalapeños, cilantro, red onion, and avocado

» **Makes enough for 4 to 6 people**

HOT SAUCE BREAD CRUMBS

1 tablespoon olive or safflower oil

2 cups chunky bread crumbs or cubes

3 tablespoons hot sauce*

1 tablespoon unsweetened plain almond milk

CHEESY SAUCE

1 tablespoon plus ¼ cup olive or safflower oil

1 shallot, chopped, or ¼ cup chopped yellow onion

2 starchy potatoes, such as russets, peeled and cubed (about 4 cups)

2 carrots, cubed (about 1½ cups)

2 cups veggie broth

1 cup unsweetened plain almond milk

½ cup nooch**

2 tablespoons lemon juice

1 tablespoon Bragg's*** or soy sauce

½ teaspoon salt

YOU'RE GODDAMN RIGHT WE MADE MAC AND CHEESE WITHOUT CHEESE. SHUT THE FUCK UP—YOU HAVEN'T EVEN TRIED IT YET. Whip up a batch of this classic comfort food and you won't ever mess with the blue and yellow boxed bullshit ever again.

CREAMY SQUASH MAC AND CHEESE WITH HOT SAUCE BREAD CRUMBS

1 First let's make the bread crumbs: Grab a large skillet with a lid (you'll see why in a bit) and warm up the oil over medium heat. Toss in the bread crumbs, stir until everything has some oil on it, and keep stirring around every few seconds until all that starts to look a little toasty, 2 to 3 minutes. In a small glass, mix together the hot sauce and milk, then pour it all over the bread crumbs, making sure everything gets coated. Remove from the heat and scrape them onto a plate. Wipe that skillet down right quick cause we're using that shit again.

2 Make the cheesy sauce: In that kinda clean skillet, warm up 1 tablespoon of the oil over medium heat. Add the shallot and sauté until it looks kinda golden, 3 to 4 minutes. Stir in the potatoes, carrots, and 1 cup of the broth. Cover and let that shit braise until the potatoes and carrots are soft, about 15 minutes. When the veggies are soft, remove from the heat and let that cool for a sec.

3 Toss the milk, nooch, lemon juice, Bragg's, salt, and remaining ¼ cup oil and 1 cup veggie broth into a blender. Add the softened veggies and all the liquids in the pan to the blender and run that shit until the sauce is all creamy, about 30 seconds.

We like Frank's RedHot but use what you've got.

**WTF? See page 189.*

***WTF? See page 188.*

4 Meanwhile, cook the pasta according to the package directions. Right before the pasta is done cooking, throw in the frozen peas. Drain the whole pot, then throw it all back into the pot and fold the squash into the pasta.

5 Pour over the warm cheesy sauce and serve right away topped with hot sauce bread crumbs.

1 pound pasta, like shells, fusilli, or anything that will hold some sauce

2 cups frozen or fresh green peas

2 cups shredded yellow squash

Got some extra time? Crank up your oven to 425°F and bake that motherfucker, bread crumbs and all, in a large baking dish until the sides start looking crispy, about 20 minutes. Totally worth the wait.

≫ **Makes enough for 6 people**

⅓ cup olive oil

4 yellow onions, thinly sliced

½ teaspoon salt

2 teaspoons sweet paprika

1 teaspoon mild chili powder

1 teaspoon smoked paprika

½ teaspoon ground cumin

¼ teaspoon ground cinnamon

3 cups shredded spinach

2 teaspoons sherry vinegar

3 cups cooked French lentils*

5 cups cooked short-grain brown rice**

There's a shitload of oil and onions here, but that's kinda this whole dish's thing, so you can't leave them out. But considering some version of this has been around since the 1200s and is eaten by millions of people all over the Arab world, maybe you're wrong and should branch the fuck out. TRY NEW SHIT, START WITH ONIONS.

MUJADDARA

1 In a large deep skillet or soup pot, warm up the oil over medium-high heat. Throw in the onions and salt and cook them, stirring often, until they're all browned and cooked down, about 20 minutes.

2 Reduce the heat to medium and add the paprika, chili powder, smoked paprika, cumin, and cinnamon. Cook for 30 seconds to let those spices really mix together, then fold in the spinach and vinegar. Let that shit cook until it gets all wilted, about 3 minutes. Fold in the lentils and rice and serve that old-school deliciousness.

* These are the dark greenish black ones at the store, they hold their shape better. No fucking clue how to cook lentils? See page 181.

** No idea? See page 182.

One-pot meals are where it's at. Fast, easy, and best of all: minimal dishes. Especially if you eat straight out of the pot you cooked everything in like a goddamn genius.

ONE-POT CHICKPEA BIRYANI

1 Cook the veggies: In a large soup pot, warm up 1 tablespoon of the coconut oil over medium heat. Add the onions and sauté until they start to brown all over, about 7 minutes. Remove them from the pot and set those bastards aside.

2 In that same pot, heat the remaining 1 tablespoon oil over medium-high heat. Toss in the cauliflower, green beans, and carrot and sauté that shit around until they start to soften up and get browned in a few spots, about 5 minutes. Fold in the chickpeas, garam masala, garlic, and ginger and cook for another minute to get the spices all mixed up. Remove from the heat, remove all the veggies from the pot, and set them off by the onions.

3 Make the rice: In that same damn pot, warm up the coconut oil over medium heat. Add the rice, cinnamon, bay leaf, garam masala, ginger, and garlic and sauté that shit until the spices start to smell all delicious, about 1 minute. Add the veggie broth and bring it all to a simmer. Reduce the heat to low, cover, and cook until the rice is tender and the liquid has evaporated, 15 to 20 minutes. Sprinkle the turmeric mixture over about half of the cooked rice and let it sit with the heat off for a minute to absorb.

4 To serve, fluff the rice with a fork, fold in the veggies, three-quarters of the onions, the nuts, and raisins. Top with some cilantro and the rest of the onions and serve that shit up right away.

* WTF? See page 188.

** We used the turmeric to give the rice its signature occasional yellow grains of rice without spending the extra cash on the traditional saffron. If you don't already have turmeric though, don't bother with this shit. It's just for looks.

COOK TIME 35 MINS

» **Makes enough for 4 to 6 people**

VEGGIES

2 tablespoons coconut oil

1 large yellow onion, halved

2 cups chopped cauliflower

1 cup chopped green beans

1 carrot, chopped

1½ cups cooked chickpeas

1 teaspoon garam masala*

1 clove garlic, minced

2 teaspoons minced fresh ginger

RICE

1 tablespoon coconut oil

2 cups basmati rice

1 cinnamon stick

1 bay leaf

1 teaspoon garam masala*

1 teaspoon minced fresh ginger

1 clove garlic, minced

4 cups vegetable broth

¼ teaspoon ground turmeric** mixed with 1 tablespoon water

¼ cup chopped cashews or almonds

¼ cup golden raisins

Chopped cilantro, for topping

COOK TIME 45 MINS

>> **Makes enough for 4 people, no fucking problem**

1 can (15 ounces) no-salt-added tomato sauce

1 can (14 ounces) whole artichoke hearts, drained and rinsed

½ yellow onion, chopped

2 cloves garlic, peeled

½ cup nooch**

3 tablespoons balsamic vinegar

½ teaspoon dried thyme

¼ teaspoon salt

1 pound dried noodley pasta, such as spaghetti or fettuccine, cooked according to package directions

1 zucchini, shredded

¼ cup thinly sliced fresh basil

2 tablespoons olive oil

½ cup bread crumbs, panko or regular

Spray oil

How can you make spaghetti even better? Bake it in to a fucking pie. Then slice that shit up and live your best life.

CRISPY SPAGHETTI PIE

1 Crank up your oven to 450°F. Grease up an 8-inch springform pan.* Wrap the bottom of that in foil in case your pan leaks.

2 In a blender or food processor, throw together the tomato sauce, artichoke hearts, onion, garlic, nooch, vinegar, thyme, and salt. Let that motherfucker rip until everything is mostly minced up and it looks kinda smooth.

3 In a big-ass bowl, mix together the cooked pasta, zucchini, basil, and olive oil until everything is coated in oil. Pour in the sauce mixture and keep tossing until everything is covered. Fold in the bread crumbs and stir until they're combined. Throw it all in your prepared pan, pressing down so that it's dense as fuck.

4 Spray the top of it with oil and then stick that shit in the oven. Bake until the top looks a little burnt and the sides are starting to pull away from the pan, 25 to 35 minutes. Let this carb cake cool for 10 minutes before slicing in.

If you don't know what a springform pan is, fucking look it up and you'll understand why that's key to this working.

*** WTF? See page 189.*

DID YOU KNOW?

The city of Mari Nara, CA, lost a combined 6,572 pounds on the famed Spaghetti Cleanse and thus became the namesake of the beloved marinara sauce. Start your spaghetti cleanse today!

WHO THE FUCK
WOULDN'T WANT
A SLICE OF
SPAGHETTI?

» WHERE TO CUT CORNERS

We try our best, but we all can't go to five different farmers' markets a day, cook everything from scratch, and still look legit. We regular folks need to figure out how to do our best in the kitchen without killing our damn selves in the process. So we're gonna let you in on our favorite store-bought ways to cut corners in the kitchen—perfect for when you have no fucks left to give but still need to make dinner. So feel no shame; our asses are lazy, too.

- » Canned beans
- » Canned pumpkin puree
- » Canned tomatoes
- » Concentrated vegetable broth mix
- » Frozen fruit
- » Frozen veggies and greens
- » Low-salt spaghetti sauce
- » Refrigerated salsa

We've eaten this for dinner waaaay too many nights to count. This is one of those "SHIT I forgot to go to the store" kinda dishes, but it tastes so good you won't care. Go ahead, give in to the lazy.

PASTA PISELLI

1 Cook the pasta according to the package directions because they know their shit. About a minute before the pasta is done cooking, throw in the peas so that they warm up. Drain the pasta and peas but save ¼ cup of the pasta water cause we're gonna use that in a sec.

2 In the pot you just used to cook the pasta, warm up the olive oil over medium heat. Add the shallot and salt and cook until the shallot starts to get translucent, about 2 minutes. Toss in the spinach and cook until it starts to wilt, another minute. Throw in the cooked pasta and peas, the Bragg's, lemon juice, and pasta water. Stir, then toss in the nooch and garlic powder and stir until everything is coated.

3 Serve right away topped with a little parsley.

* All this shit is optional. If you don't have it, leave it out and it will still taste legit.

** WTF? See page 188.

*** WTF? See page 189.

COOK TIME 15 MINS

›› **Makes enough for 2 to 4 people**

1 pound dried stubby pasta, such as elbow macaroni or shells

3½ cups frozen peas (one 16-ounce bag)

2 tablespoons olive oil

1 shallot, diced, or ¼ cup diced onion*

Pinch of salt

3 cups chopped spinach or kale*

2 tablespoons Bragg's** or soy sauce

2 tablespoons lemon juice

¼ cup nooch***

⅛ teaspoon garlic powder

Parsley, for garnish*

» **Makes enough for 4 people**

1 pound linguine or other long-as-fuck noodle

BALSAMIC-GLAZED CHICKPEAS

1 tablespoon olive oil

1½ cups cooked chickpeas or 1 can (15 ounces), drained and rinsed

2 tablespoons balsamic vinegar

¼ teaspoon garlic powder

SWISS CHARD AND TOMATO SAUCE

1 tablespoon olive oil

1 bunch Swiss chard, sliced crosswise into ½-inch-wide ribbons, rib and all*

2 to 3 cloves garlic, you do you

⅔ cup white wine**

¼ teaspoon salt

1 can (15 ounces) diced tomatoes

¼ teaspoon red pepper flakes

¼ cup sliced Kalamata olives

1 tablespoon balsamic vinegar

Had to grab this one off the blog because we get so many comments on it. Make this shit for yourself and see what all the buzz is about.

SWISS CHARD AND TOMATO LINGUINE WITH BALSAMIC-GLAZED CHICKPEAS

1 First, put on a big pot of water and cook the pasta according to the package directions. Simple shit.

2 To make the glazed chickpeas: Warm up the olive oil in a large soup pot over medium heat. (Yeah, it seems kinda big, but you're gonna use that shit for the sauce later and we're too lazy to have multiple dirty pots, so just trust us.) Add the chickpeas and sauté them around until they are all warmed up and kinda starting to sizzle, 2 to 3 minutes. Pour in the balsamic and continue gently stirring all that shit around until most of the liquid has evaporated, another 2 to 3 minutes. Sprinkle in the garlic powder and remove from the heat. Pour the chickpeas into a bowl.

3 Make the sauce: Just quickly rinse out that same pot a little bit with some water, then warm up the olive oil. Add the Swiss chard and stir it around so a little oil gets on all of it. Yeah, it looks like way too fucking much chard, but this shit is gonna cook down, so just keep stirring it for about 3 minutes until it's all wilted. Add the garlic, white wine, and salt, and cook for another 2 minutes. Add the can of diced tomatoes, juice and all that shit, and the pepper flakes and cook until the chard is cooked all the way down and tastes tender, 3 to 5 minutes.

4 Fold the cooked pasta into the sauce and cook it for another minute so the pasta can absorb some of the sauce. Remove from the heat and fold in the olives and balsamic vinegar. Taste and add more garlic, pepper flakes, whateverthefuck you like. See? That shit was easy even if you're sipping from the wine bottle the whole time.

5 Serve right away, topped with the chickpeas, and with a glass of the rest of that white wine and have yourself one relaxing-ass evening.

* This is roughly 8 cups.

** If you aren't a wine person, just replace it with veggie broth. Def don't recommend sipping broth from the bottle though.

>> **Makes enough for 4 people**

1 teaspoon plus
1 tablespoon
safflower oil

1 large carrot,
chopped

1 leek, chopped

⅛ teaspoon Chinese
5-spice powder

3 cups cooked barley
(page 183), cooled for
several hours in the
fridge

2 tablespoons tamari

1 tablespoon rice
vinegar

2 cups spinach,
chopped

1 cup frozen green
peas (unthawed is
cool)

⅓ cup chopped green
onions

Sure, there's no rice in here, but when the fuck did that become a deal breaker? Think for yourselves, sheeple.

LEEK AND BARLEY "FRIED RICE"

I In a large wok or skillet, heat 1 teaspoon of the oil over medium heat. Add the carrot and leek and stir-fry those stalky fuckers until they begin to get golden in some spots, about 5 minutes. Add the 5-spice powder, stir that shit up, and remove all that from the pan.

2 Throw the pan back on the stove over medium heat and warm up the remaining 1 tablespoon oil. Add the barley and stir-fry it up until it begins to get warm, about 3 minutes. Add the tamari, rice vinegar, cooked vegetables, spinach, and peas and stir-fry it all for an additional couple of minutes until everything is mixed up, the spinach wilted as fuck, and the peas warmed up. Fold in the chopped green onions.

3 Remove from the heat and serve immediately.

This simple pot of rice is so legit that sometimes we crave just this and some black beans for dinner. If you want a more impressive meal, throw this shit in your Borracho Squash and Bean Burritos (page 104) and eat your damn heart out.

COCONUT-LIME RICE

COOK TIME 40 MINS

>> **Makes about 6 cups**

2 tablespoons coconut oil*

2 cups brown rice

1 tablespoon grated lime zest

2 cloves garlic, minced

4 cups vegetable broth

¼ teaspoon salt

2 tablespoons lime juice

½ cup chopped cilantro (optional)

1 Heat the oil in a large saucepan over medium heat. Add the rice and sauté that shit until it smells a little nutty, about 2 minutes. Add the lime zest and stir it all up so that it doesn't just sit in a clump in the damn pot the whole time. Throw in the garlic, broth, and salt and stir again. Bring to a simmer, then reduce the heat, cover, and let this very softly simmer until all the broth is absorbed and the rice is tender, about 35 minutes.

2 When the rice is tender, remove from the heat and fold in the lime juice and cilantro (if using). Serve warm.

We like unrefined coconut oil here because it tastes the most coconutty (fancy culinary term) and we're into that.

DID YOU KNOW?

Despite both belonging to the citrus family, limes and lemons are *not* the same goddamn thing. REMEMBER THAT SHIT. Talkin' to you, bartender who tried to put a slice of lemon in our gin and tonics.

COOK TIME 35 MINS

>> **Makes enough for 8 burritos, no fucking problem**

FILLING

1 tablespoon olive oil

1 yellow or white onion, chopped

3 cups peeled, chopped butternut squash*

1 jalapeño, minced

1 tablespoon mild chili powder

1 teaspoon smoked paprika

1 tablespoon Bragg's**

¾ cup beer (your favorite)***

2 cloves garlic, minced

3 cups cooked pinto beans or 2 cans (15 ounces each), drained and rinsed

2 tablespoons lime juice

2 tablespoons pure maple syrup or whatever liquid sweetener you're about

BURRITOS

8 flour tortillas

Coconut-Lime Rice (page 103)

Midsummer Salsa from *Thug Kitchen: Eat Like You Give a Fuck* or whatever salsa you like

Lettuce

Avocado

Cilantro

Ever been drunk and said "I just want, like, a big-ass burrito"? Well this recipe satisfies that late-night urge, sober or not. However, we highly recommend working with heat and sharp knives prior to getting shitfaced.

BORRACHO SQUASH AND BEAN BURRITOS

1 Make the filling: In a large, deep skillet, warm up the olive oil over medium heat. Add the onion and let that cook until it gets kinda golden, 3 to 4 minutes. Add the squash, jalapeño, chili powder, and smoked paprika and stir it all round for about a minute. Pour in the Bragg's and beer and sprinkle in the garlic. Cover that shit, reduce the heat to medium-low, and simmer everything together until the squash is soft enough you can stick a fork in it, about 20 minutes.

2 When it's good to go, uncover, fold in the beans, then add the lime juice and maple syrup. Stir it all together and let it simmer until all the extra liquid has evaporated and the beans have warmed up, about 2 more minutes. Remove from the heat.

3 Make some goddamn burritos: We like them with coconut-lime rice (page 103), some salsa, lettuce, avocado, and cilantro with a bottle of hot sauce on the side, but you do you. You should know what the fuck you like in a burrito.

You can use pumpkin or whateverthefuck winter squash you find on sale.

** *WTF? See page 188.*

*** *As long as it's something you'd drink eating a burrito, you should be all right.*

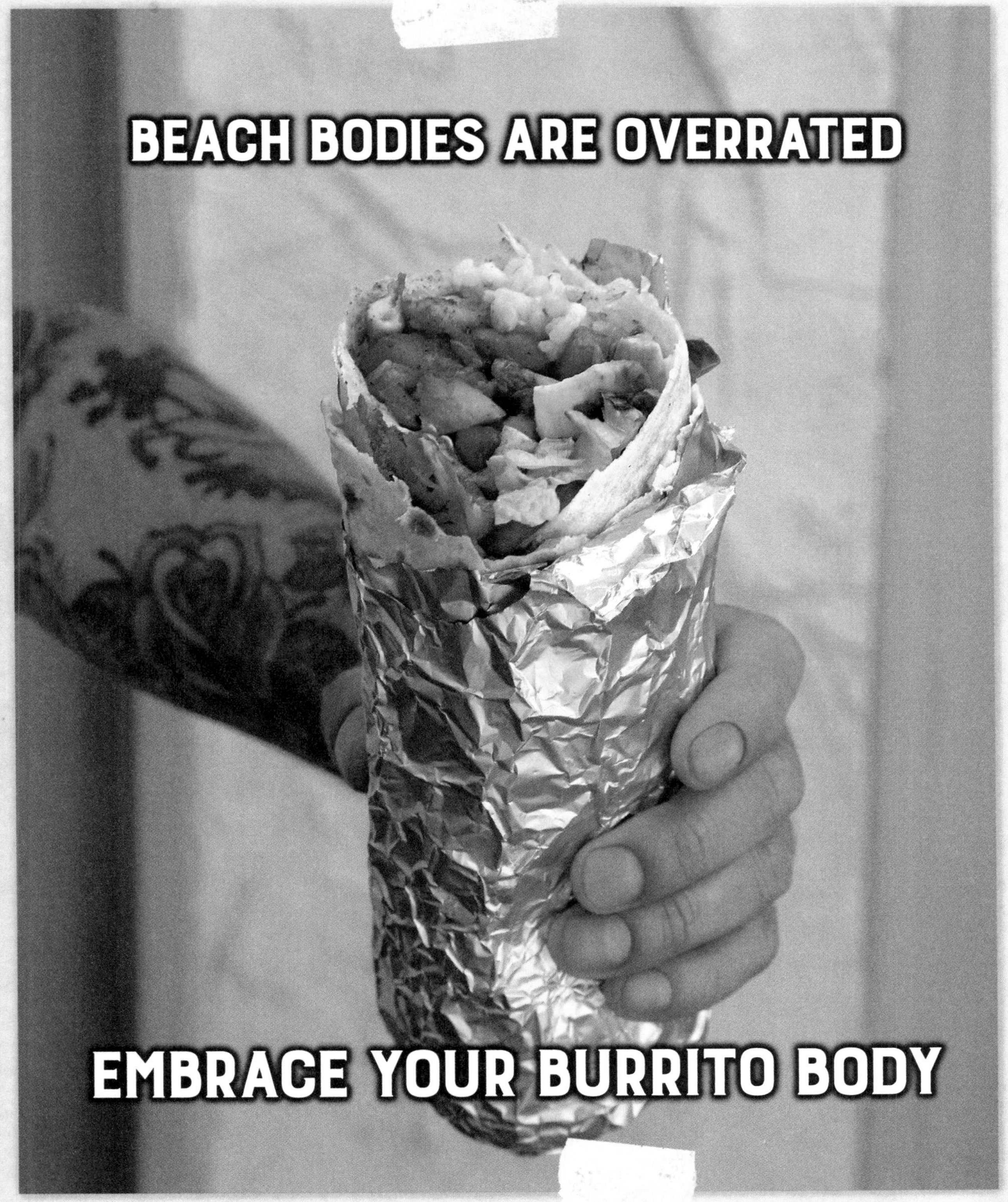
BEACH BODIES ARE OVERRATED
EMBRACE YOUR BURRITO BODY

Got leftovers of the Protein-Packed Mixed Herb Tabbouleh Salad (page 50) that you're about to stash in the back of the fridge? Hold up, just add a few more ingredients and you've got some motherfucking falafel and a whole new dinner. Best thing? You can use this technique with any kind of bean or grain salad leftovers. BOOM.

CLEAN-OUT-THE-FRIDGE FALAFEL

1 Heat your oven to 375°F. Grab and grease a rimmed baking sheet.

2 Mash up the chickpeas with a potato masher or big fucking spoon in a large bowl until there are no large chunks left. Fold in the leftover salad, onion, olive oil, cumin, garlic, and salt and stir it up. Add the bread crumbs and stir again so that it's all mixed in.

3 To make the falafel, grab about ¼ cup of the mixture and roll it between your hands to form a ball about the size of a golf ball. If the mixture is sticking to your hands, don't freak out and just wet them under the tap and get back to rolling.

4 Place the balls on the baking sheet and spray the tops lightly with oil. Bake until both sides are kinda golden, 25 to 30 minutes, flipping halfway.

5 Serve in a pita with all your favorite stuff or over a salad. Either way, pour on some tahini sauce for a good time.

* Using a 15-ounce can is always fine.

COOK TIME 35 MINS

>> **Makes about 18 pieces of falafel**

1½ cups cooked chickpeas*

3 cups Protein-Packed Mixed Herb Tabbouleh Salad (page 50)

½ cup chopped yellow onion

1 tablespoon olive oil

1½ teaspoons ground cumin

1 clove garlic, minced

Pinch of salt

½ cup bread crumbs, like the kind you buy in the store

Spray oil

FOR SERVING
Pita bread

Spinach

Onions, sliced

Tomatoes, chopped

Cucumber, chopped

Tahini Sauce (page 198)

>> **Makes enough for 2 to 4 people**

2 tablespoons olive oil

½ white onion, thinly slivered

1 pound angel hair pasta

2 cups chopped spinach

2 cloves garlic, minced

1 teaspoon ground cumin

¼ teaspoon salt

1 can (15 ounces) no-salt-added tomato sauce

4 cups vegetable broth

¼ teaspoon garlic powder

2 tablespoons lime juice

⅓ cup chopped cilantro

There are a bazillion different ways to cook fideo, but this is how we like it best, more of a pasta and less of a soup. This comes together real quick but the flavor makes it seem like you put in way more effort than you actually did. You could pair this shit with Chipotle Caesar Salad (page 32) for a really dope but simple dinner.

FIDEO

1 Warm up the olive oil in a large soup pot over medium heat. Add the onion and sauté that shit around for a minute. With the pasta still in its container, start crunching that bastard up with your hands into bite-size pieces as you add it to the pot. You don't want pieces larger than 3 inches long if you can help it. Sauté all that around until the pasta gets a little oil on all of it, about 2 minutes.

2 Add the spinach, garlic, cumin, and salt and stir it around so everything isn't just fucking clumped together. Add the tomato sauce, broth, and garlic powder and stir it to make sure the pasta is covered. Let that all simmer together, stirring on occasion, until the pasta is tender, 5 to 7 minutes.

3 Remove from the heat and fold in the lime juice and cilantro. Serve right away.

Stop boiling Brussels sprouts and start roasting those little fuckers—it'll change your whole perspective on shit like sun bathing off the southern coast of St. Bart's with spider monkeys.

SHREDDED BRUSSELS SPROUTS AND QUINOA PILAF

1 Crank up your oven to 425°F.

2 Pour the Brussels sprouts, shallot, garlic, olive oil, lemon juice, curry powder, and salt into a baking dish and mix until everything is coated. Toss it in the oven until everything looks golden, about 20 minutes, stirring halfway through.

3 Let the Brussels sprouts cool for a couple minutes, then pour them into a medium bowl with the quinoa, chives, nuts, and dried fruit (if you're using that shit). Serve warm or let that chill out in the fridge a bit. Best served the day it's made.

* No fucking clue? See page 183.

COOK TIME 25 MINS

» **Makes enough for 2 to 4 as a side**

1 pound Brussels sprouts, shredded or thinly sliced (about 5 cups)

1 shallot, chopped, or ¼ cup chopped yellow onion

1 clove garlic, minced

1 tablespoon olive oil

2 teaspoons lemon juice

½ teaspoon curry powder

Pinch of salt

1½ cups cooked quinoa*

½ cup chopped chives or green onions

½ cup chopped toasted nuts, such as almonds or walnuts

¼ cup golden raisins or currants (optional)

COOK TIME 25 MINS

>> **Makes enough for 4 people**

9 ounces noodles, such as udon

4 heads baby bok choy, cut lengthwise into thin strips

SESAME SAUCE

¼ cup tahini*

½ cup vegetable broth or water, warmed

2 tablespoons rice vinegar

1 tablespoon soy sauce or tamari

1 tablespoon hot chili oil**

1 teaspoon agave or your favorite liquid sweetener

1 clove garlic, minced

¼ teaspoon Chinese 5-spice powder

1 tablespoon safflower, grapeseed, or other neutral oil

8 ounces tempeh*

1 shallot, diced

1 tablespoon minced fresh ginger

⅛ teaspoon Chinese 5-spice powder

1 tablespoon rice vinegar

2 teaspoons soy sauce or tamari

Toppings: green onions, sliced cucumbers, toasted sesame seeds, toasted peanuts

This tasty dish used to be peddled by street vendors to busy people back in the day, so it's basically OG food truck grub. Make this at home and get all the flavor without all the hipsters.

DAN DAN NOODLES

1 Stick a large soup pot of water on the stove for the noodles and get it boiling over medium heat. Cook the noodles according to whatever the package directions say but just be sure to throw in the bok choy during the last minute of the pasta cooking. Drain and then run it under cool water so the bok choy stays looking bright green.

2 While that shit is cooking, make the sesame sauce: Mix together the tahini, broth, vinegar, soy sauce, chili oil, and agave in a medium glass until it looks all smooth and mixed up. Stir in the garlic and 5-spice powder, then set that shit aside.

3 In a wok or medium skillet, warm up the safflower oil over medium heat. Crumble in the tempeh in bite-size pieces and sauté it around until it starts to brown, about 4 minutes. Add the shallot and ginger and cook for a minute longer to give the shallot time to soften up. Add the 5-spice powder, vinegar, and soy sauce and cook for another minute to let everything absorb. Remove from the heat.

4 To assemble the bowl, pour one-quarter of the sesame sauce in the bottom of each bowl, add some noodles and baby bok choy, drizzle on a little more sauce, then top with the tempeh and whatever other topping you wanna throw at it. Serve warm or chilled, your call. This shit is great as leftovers, so double up and take to work for lunch.

* WTF? See page 189.

** Can't find? Just use toasted sesame oil and squirt in some Sriracha if you want some heat.

NEXT TIME SOMEONE
ASKS YOU FOR NOODS
SEXT THIS

If you can make a stir fry, you can make this shit. Exorcise your dietary demons with this Korean classic.

JAPCHAE

1 Cook the noodles according to the package directions. Drain that shit and set aside.

2 Mix together the soy sauce, vinegar, water, and chili paste in a small glass and set aside.

3 Warm the sesame oil up in a large wok or skillet over medium-high heat. Throw in the white onion, carrots, and bell pepper and cook until everything starts to soften, 2 to 3 minutes. Toss in the mushrooms and cook for a minute more.

4 Fold in the noodles and add the reserved sauce mixture and keep tossing them around for about another minute till everything gets all mixed up and nothing sticks to the pan. Fold in the greens and cook until they start to wilt, 1 to 2 minutes.

5 Remove from the heat, taste, and add more of whateverthefuck you think it needs. Top with toasted sesame seeds and serve it up right away.

ROADSIDE ASSISTANCE Wanna make it a meal? Add some edamame or Dry-Fried Tofu (page 200).

COOK TIME 15 MINS

》 **Makes enough for 4 to 6 people, or 1 person all damn week**

12 ounces sweet potato, mung, or thin rice noodles

¼ cup soy sauce or tamari

3 tablespoons rice vinegar

2 tablespoons water

1 tablespoon garlic chili paste

2 tablespoons toasted sesame oil

1 small white onion, slivered

2 carrots, cut into matchsticks

1 red bell pepper, cut into matchsticks

2 cups sliced shiitake or button mushrooms

4 cups chopped greens, such as bok choy, spinach, or kale

Toasted sesame seeds, for garnish

COOK TIME 25 MINS

>> **Makes enough for 4 to 6 people**

1 pound noodley pasta, such as linguine

SAUCE

3 tablespoons olive oil

½ white or yellow onion, chopped

1 rib celery, chopped

1 carrot, chopped

1 cup minced cremini or button mushrooms

¼ teaspoon salt

1 clove garlic, minced

½ teaspoon dried oregano

½ teaspoon dried basil

Dash of red pepper flakes, if you can hang

½ cup red wine*

1 tablespoon tomato paste

1½ cups no-salt-added tomato sauce**

1½ cups cooked chickpeas, chopped***

Chopped parsley, for garnish

Sure, bolognese is usually made with ground beef, but we'll take a hard pass on that questionable pink slime. We're ride or die for chickpeas, our main chick(pea).

CHICKPEA BOLOGNESE

1 Cook the pasta according to the package directions, they know what the fuck they're talking about. Drain it when you're done and set it aside.

2 While the pasta is cooking, make the sauce: In a large, deep skillet or wok, heat the oil over medium heat. Add the onion, celery, and carrot and cook for 5 minutes so that they start to soften up and get kinda golden in some spots. Add the mushrooms and salt and cook for another 2 minutes. Stir in the garlic, herbs, and pepper flakes, then pour in the wine. Sauté for another 2 minutes while the wine cooks down a bit. Then stir in the tomato paste and sauce. Bring all that to a gentle simmer and then fold in the chickpeas.

3 Reduce the heat under the sauce to low and toss in the pasta. When everything is all cooked in the sauce turn off the heat. Serve hot topped with some chopped parsley.

Just use whatever you wanna drink with the dish. No adult beverages tonight? Just add veggie broth instead.

**One 15-ounce can. Don't buy anything with a fuckton of salt or unnecessary spices in it. Just the plainest shit you can find.*

***One 15-ounce can, drained, is fine. If you have a food processor, just pulse them a couple times so two-thirds of them are kinda chopped up. Otherwise just kinda rough-chop them with a knife to about the size of a watermelon seed.*

SERVING SIZES ARE
SUBJECTIVE

>> **Makes enough for 4 people**

2 tablespoons safflower or grapeseed oil

2 cloves garlic, chopped

1 tablespoon minced fresh ginger

3 tablespoons red curry paste*

3 cups vegetable broth

1 can (15 ounces) coconut milk

1 tablespoon soy sauce or tamari

12 ounces dried rice vermicelli noodles, cooked according to the package directions

4 cups chopped spinach

Dry-Fried Tofu (page 200)

2 tablespoons lime juice

Toppings: sliced red onion, chopped cilantro and green onions

Lime wedges, for squeezing

Can't afford a vacation? How about a taste-cation? (We know that was really fucking lame, but our publisher said we had to write something.)

RED CURRY NOODLES

In a large pot, heat the oil, garlic, ginger, and red curry paste over medium heat and cook them all together for 2 minutes to wake up all that flavor in the curry paste. Add the veggie broth, coconut milk, and soy sauce. Bring it all to a boil, then fold in the noodles, spinach, tofu, and lime juice. Simmer that all up until the spinach has wilted, about 2 minutes. Remove from the heat and taste to see if it's where you like it. Serve it up with all the toppings and the lime wedges and get down on some good shit.

You can find this in a glass or small can near the coconut milk and soy sauce in the store. It's full of shallots, lemongrass, galangal, and red chiles, among other things. Some pastes are hotter than others, so try 1 tablespoon first and then work your way up in the recipe. There are hundreds of recipes for this shit, so if you have a well-stocked store, look one up online and make it from scratch.

THUG KITCHEN AIR
1ST CLASS BAGGAGE
Name _Hal Apeno_
Address _101 E. Fork_
City _Santa Monica_
State _California_
INSPECTED AND APPROVED

Polenta is too versatile to restrict to just being a breakfast food. This dish combines polenta's creaminess with the savory puttanesca sauce to make a dinner so dope, don't be surprised if your family leaves a tip at the table. KEEP THAT SHIT. YOU EARNED IT.

POLENTA PUTTANESCA

1 First let's make the polenta: Grab a large pot and bring the broth and milk to a boil over medium heat. Gently whisk in the polenta a little at a time and add the salt. (If you just dump all the cornmeal in there at once, it'll get clumpy and you already fucked up so don't do that.) Bring it all to a boil, then reduce that heat to low. Cover the pot and let that deliciousness simmer for 15 to 25 minutes. Stir it on occasion while you work on the sauce because if it gets too hot, it's gonna stick to the bottom and you don't want that.

2 Now we're gonna make the puttanesca sauce: Warm up the olive oil in a large skillet over medium heat. Throw in the garlic, capers, oregano, and red pepper flakes and sauté that shit around until the garlic looks kinda golden, about 2 minutes. Add the tomatoes and their juices to the pot, crushing the tomatoes with your hands as you add them if you bought them whole. Fold in the olives and let that shit cook together over medium-low heat, stirring occasionally, until the polenta is ready. Easy.

3 When the polenta has absorbed most of the liquid and is tender, remove from the heat and stir in the nooch. Serve it up right away and top with sauce and some parsley or basil and whateverthefuck else you want. Sprinkle actual sprinkles if you want, get fucking weird with it.

* WTF? See page 189.

** These picked motherfuckers are near the olives at the store. They sound all fancy but one jar will last you forever, cost you about $5 bucks, and really class up your fridge.

》 **Makes enough for 4 hungry people**

POLENTA

3½ cups vegetable broth

3 cups unsweetened nondairy milk like almond

1½ cups polenta or yellow grits

¼ teaspoon salt

¼ cup nooch*

PUTTANESCA SAUCE

3 tablespoons olive oil

3 cloves garlic, minced

2 tablespoons drained capers**

1 teaspoon dried oregano

½ teaspoon red pepper flakes

1 can (28 ounces) whole tomatoes in juice or crushed tomatoes

½ cup pitted Kalamata olives

Toppings: chopped parsley or basil, nooch, red pepper flakes

1. **Polenta Puttanesca** (page 117)
2. **Basil**
3. **Wine**
4. **Entrance to a Key Party**

1. **Quinoa Taco Mix**
   (page 122)

2. **Sweet Potato Al Pastor**

3. **Jason coming for some tacos**

Wanna stuff your face with tacos but without the guilt? We got you. These al pastor tacos pack a flavorful punch that's only surpassed by the fuckload of fiber packed into every bite. Eat 10 tacos but with the healthy sense of satisfaction you get from eating salad.

COOK TIME 15 MINS

SWEET POTATO AL PASTOR

1 Make the filling: In a blender or food processor, throw together the onion, pineapple, lime juice, chili powder, liquid smoke, smoked paprika, cumin, and oregano. Let that motherfucker rip until the sauce starts looking sorta smooth, then set aside.

2 In a large skillet, warm the oil up over medium heat. Add the tempeh and sauté it around for about 2 minutes, then fold in the sweet potato and sprinkle over the Bragg's. Keep cooking until the sweet potato starts to soften up, 3 to 5 minutes longer.

3 Pour in the sauce you blended up earlier and stir it all up until everything is covered and starting to warm up, about 3 more minutes. Remove from the heat.

4 Start making some damn tacos: Warm the tortillas and serve topped with the filling, onions, jalapeños, and cilantro, or pineapple salsa.

* WTF? See page 188.

** WTF? See page 189.

>> **Makes enough for 8 good-size tacos, enough for 4 to 6 people**

FILLING

½ white onion, chopped

1 cup fresh or canned pineapple chunks with ¼ cup juice

¼ cup lime juice

3 tablespoons mild chili powder

2 teaspoons liquid smoke*

2 teaspoons smoked paprika

1 teaspoon ground cumin

½ teaspoon dried oregano

2 tablespoons olive or safflower oil

8 ounces tempeh,** cut into thin 1-inch-long strips

3 cups shredded raw sweet potato

2 tablespoons Bragg's* or soy sauce

TACOS

8 corn tortillas

Toppings: diced onion, jalapeños, cilantro, Pineapple Salsa (page 21)

》 **Makes enough for 4 to 6 people**

FILLING

2 tablespoons olive oil

½ medium yellow onion, chopped

1 red bell pepper, diced

1 jalapeño, seeded and minced

2 cups cooked quinoa*

1 clove garlic, minced

1 tablespoon chili powder

½ teaspoon ground cumin

¼ teaspoon smoked paprika

1½ cups cooked black beans, crushed with a potato masher or pulsed in the food processor for 5 seconds

1 tablespoon lime juice

2 tablespoons Bragg's** or soy sauce

TACOS

8 corn tortillas

Toppings: Midsummer Salsa from *Thug Kitchen: Eat Like You Give a Fuck*, shredded lettuce, diced red onion, Everyday Guacamole from *Thug Kitchen Party Grub*

Packed with two sources of protein and a fuckton of spices, this taco mix is good folded into tacos or flautas, sprinkled over nachos, or just eaten out of the pan with a spoon. Consider making a double batch and just stick the rest in the freezer so you can have a bomb-ass dinner ready in 5 minutes when you've got no energy to cook. Which is probably always but whatever. Just make this.

QUINOA TACO MIX

1 Make the filling: Warm the oil in a large skillet over medium-high heat. Add the onion and bell pepper and sauté until the onion starts to brown, about 5 minutes. Add the jalapeño, quinoa, and garlic and cook for another minute. Sprinkle in the chili powder, cumin, and smoked paprika and stir until everything is coated, then cook for another minute. Your place should smell pretty fucking dope right about now. Fold in the mashed black beans, lime juice, and Bragg's, and cook just long enough to warm up the beans while lightly stirring, about another minute. No need to mash that shit up anymore. Remove from the heat.

2 Put together some motherfucking tacos: Throw that mix on a corn tortilla with some pico de gallo, lettuce, onion, and guacamole and get down. Serve right away. Leftovers are great on some nachos, just sayin' . . .

* *No clue? See page 183.*

** *WTF? See page 188.*

NACHOS? YOU MEAN
CHIP SALAD?

COOK TIME 25 MINS

>> **Makes about 2½ cups**

1 tablespoon olive or safflower oil

1 shallot, chopped or ¼ cup chopped yellow onion

1 clove garlic, minced

2 starchy potatoes like russets, peeled and cubed (4 cups)

2 carrots, peeled and cubed (1½ cups)

2 cups veggie broth, divided

1 cup unsweetened almond milk

½ cup nooch*

¼ cup olive or safflower oil

2 tablespoons lime juice

1 tablespoon Bragg's**

½ teaspoons salt

1 teaspoon chili powder

½ teaspoon cumin

1½ cups diced canned tomatoes

1 jalapeño, seeded and minced

Toppings: chips, red onion, cilantro, jalapeño slices, Quinoa Taco Mix (previous page) or 1½ cups cooked black beans, Midsummer Salsa from *Thug Kitchen: Eat Like You Give a Fuck*, and Everyday Guacamole from *Thug Kitchen Party Grub*

This is the dinner you have when you just want to LIVE. Go ahead, put on your sweatpants and get ready to not sweat.

NACHOS WITH TEX-MEX QUESO

1 In a clean skillet warm the tablespoon of oil of the over a medium heat. Add the shallot and sauté until it looks kinda golden, 3 to 4 minutes. Add the garlic, potatoes, carrots, and first cup of broth to the pan, stir, then cover. Let that shit braise until the potatoes and carrots are soft, about 15 minutes. When the veggies are soft, let that cool for a sec while you toss the rest of the veggie broth, milk, nooch, oil, lime juice, Bragg's, salt, and spices into a blender. Add the softened veggies and all the liquids in the pan to the blender and run that shit until the sauce is all creamy, about 30 seconds. Taste and add more spices or lime juice if you think that shit is necessary. Stir in the tomatoes and jalapeño, DO NOT BLEND, taste and then serve that shit right away as a dip or go ahead and make the damn nachos.

2 To make the nachos warm up your oven to 350 degrees and line a large baking sheet with tortilla chips. Drizzle the chips with ½ cup of the queso and 1 cup of the Quinoa Taco Mix. Add another layer of chips, queso, and taco mix and then stick that shit in oven until the chips are all warmed up, about 10 minutes. Layer on the salsa, cilantro, onions, jalapeños, guacamole, and more queso and Quinoa Taco Mix. You know how the fuck to make nachos. Serve this tasty son of a bitch right away and brace yourself for some next level nacho-ness.

* WTF? See page 189.

** WTF? See page 188.

A friend brought a dish like this to a potluck one time and we loved it so much we had to come up with our own version. Candice, thanks for the inspiration. We owe you a beer.

SHREDDED APPLE POLENTA WITH DILL

1 First let's make the polenta. Grab a large pot and bring the broth and milk to a boil over medium heat. Gently whisk in the polenta a little at a time, then add the garlic and salt. (If you just dump all the cornmeal in there at once, it'll get clumpy, you'll get frustrated, and one of you will get burnt in the process.) Bring it all to a boil, then reduce that heat to low. Cover the pot and let that deliciousness simmer for 15 to 25 minutes. Stir occasionally cause it's gonna stick to the bottom if you don't and cleaning that pot is no fucking fun.

2 When the polenta has absorbed most of the liquid and is tender, remove from the heat and stir in the oil, nooch, apple, chives, dill, and lemon juice. Taste and add pepper if that's your thing. Serve it up right away and top with some more chives and dill if you've got 'em.

* WTF? See page 189.

** We like Granny Smith here, but you can use anything as long as it isn't too sweet. Just leave the skin on and take that shit right to the side of your box grater. It usually takes 1 fist-size apple to get a cup.

COOK TIME 35 MINS

» **Makes enough for 4 hungry people**

3½ cups vegetable broth

3 cups unsweetened nondairy milk

1½ cups polenta or yellow grits

2 cloves garlic, minced

¼ teaspoon salt

2 tablespoons olive oil

⅓ cup nooch*

1 cup shredded apple**

¼ cup chopped chives

⅓ cup chopped fresh dill

1 tablespoon lemon juice

Dash of ground pepper

CRUISE CONTROL

SMOOTHIES, DRINKS, AND COCKTAILS

FOOD EXITS

PINEAPPLE-CUCUMBER SLUSHIE	131
APOLLO'S FURY	132
JADE 'N' JUICE	135
INSTANT OATMEAL SMOOTHIE	136
SPECIAL SAUCEY	138
DIRTY DIANNE	141
MALHOTRA MUDDLE	142
MYRAJITO	145
HOT CHOCOLATE MIX	146
AMBER WAVES	149
GINGER FIZZ	150
LAZY SUSAN	151
CHERRY JINDRA	152

40 MPH

EDIBLE
AIR CONDITIONING

If we didn't have your attention with slushie, move the fuck on. For those still reading, on a hot summer day this drink is like a private resort for your taste buds. The beach, however, is not nude so keep your fucking clothes on, weirdo.

PINEAPPLE-CUCUMBER SLUSHIE

Throw everything into a blender and run that until it's smooth. Gotta shitty blender? Just add more juice ¼ cup at a time until you get that fucker dancing for ya. Serve right away, obvs.

ROADSIDE ASSISTANCE Feel like getting a lil slushie yourself? Add 6 ounces of rum to the blender. After all, you can't spell slushie without lush.

COOK TIME 3 MINS

>> **Makes enough for 4 to 6 people**

6 cups chopped frozen pineapple

1 English cucumber, peeled and chopped (about 2½ cups)

1 cup ice cubes

15–20 mint leaves

1½ cups pineapple juice, coconut water, or white grape juice

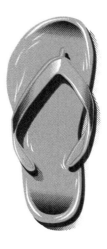

COOK TIME 3 MINS

>> **Makes 2 drinks**

2 tablespoons lime juice

2 teaspoons habañero hot sauce

½ cup white rum

¾ cup cola

½ cup club soda

We knew this one motherfucker, Apollo, who tore his ACL twice jumping off roofs, pissed on everything at his parents' house, and generally terrorized the whole block. The only reason he was never arrested was because he's a goddamn cat.

APOLLO'S FURY

Divide the lime juice between 2 glasses. Add a few ice cubes, then one of the spent lime rinds (one per glass). Add the hot sauce and rum and then stir. Pour in the cola and club soda, add a few more ice cubes, and serve right away.

DID YOU KNOW?

A doctor has determined that California is the only state in the country that knows how to party.

Worked this one up for my girl Jade so she could share it with her son Caden. We tried our best, but nothing's as sweet as that little nugget. Hopefully he'll start helping out with all these dirty dishes soon.

JADE 'N' JUICE

Throw all that shit in the blender and run until it's all smooth. Shitty blender? We've been there. Add more water ¼ cup at a time to get it going.

>> **Makes enough for 4 people or 1 crazy motherfucker**

2 bananas, cut into chunks and frozen

1 avocado

1 cup frozen strawberries

½ cup rolled oats

2 cups torn kale leaves (ribs removed)

1 cup orange or other sweet citrus juice

2 cups coconut water or tap water

COOK TIME 3 MINS

» **Makes 2 drinks**

2 cups rolled oats

2 cups unsweetened plain almond milk

2 bananas, cut into chunks and frozen

¼ cup peanut butter

8 ice cubes

2 pitted dates*

Dash of ground cinnamon

Packed with fiber and a dash of protein, this shit works as a breakfast shake or a hearty dessert. Bottoms up, bitches.

INSTANT OATMEAL SMOOTHIE

Throw the oats, almond milk, frozen banana chunks, peanut butter, ice cubes, and dates (if using) into the blender and run that son of a bitch until everything looks kind of smooth and tasty as fuck. Serve right away with a dash of cinnamon on top so that your shit looks classy.

* Optional but goddamn delicious if you're trying to make this more of a dessert.

» WHATEVERTHEFUCK FRUIT SMOOTHIE

Listen, whoever said you could only put the freshest fruit and most perfect greens into your smoothies is a goddamn liar. You're about to puree the fuck outta them, so who gives a shit if the apple is bruised and the greens are wilted? Smoothies are the best way to use up those fruits and veggies that get lost in the back of the fridge without being the asshole who just throws them away. Don't be a monster; use this guide and get blending. » **Makes 2 smoothies**

---

3 cups greens like spinach, kale, romaine, or green leaf lettuce (or a combo of these)

2 cups creamy fruit like bananas, mangos, or avocados

1½ cups tap or coconut water

1 peeled orange or ½ cup orange juice

1 cup random fruit that goes with your other choices*

Throw all that in a blender and let it do its thing. Taste and add more of whatever you want. If you want your smoothie to be thicker, add more creamy fruit (or ice in a pinch). This is obviously the kind of thing you eat right away, so slam it down as soon as it's ready.

* Any frozen fruit is legit here, but so are grapes, apples, pears, or whatever shit you've got that's a little over-the-hill.

COOK TIME 3 MINS

>> **Makes 2 drinks**

¾ **cup vodka**

6 tablespoons coffee liqueur such as Kahlúa (yeah it's dairy-free)

6 tablespoons almond or other nondairy creamer

Dark chocolate, for garnish

You ever have one of those days when you're kicked out of the bowling finals because your friend Walter was waving a fucking gun down at the lanes, your car gets set on fire, your homie Donnie dies from a heart attack, Malibu's police chief throws a mug in your face, and you're just trying to get your stolen rug back? We get it, man. We fucking get it.

SPECIAL SAUCEY

Fill 2 short glasses with ice. Divide the vodka, liqueur, and creamer evenly between the glasses. Grate some dark chocolate over each glass if you want to really tie the drink together. Serve right away.

"THE FUCK YOU WANT
ME TO SAY ABOUT IT?"
—DIANNE

This drink is dedicated to Dianne from Houston, who's simultaneously one of the freshest and dirtiest around. This drink can't do justice to what a dope person Dianne is, but she did give this recipe her seal of "SHIT that's good" approval. See Dianne? Told you we'd put you in the motherfucking book. STARTED IN THE CITY, NOW WE'RE HERE.

DIRTY DIANNE

In a big jar with a tight-fitting lid, throw the rosemary, about a cup of ice, all the juices, and the vodka. Shake the shit out of it so that the rosemary gets all bruised by the ice and releases some of its oils. Then strain out the ice and the rosemary and pour the drink into 2 glasses with a fresh sprig of rosemary stuffed in.

COOK
TIME
3
MINS

>> **Makes 2 drinks**

3 sprigs fresh rosemary, plus more for garnish

Ice

⅔ cup pineapple juice

⅓ cup orange juice

2 tablespoons lemon juice

1 cup vodka

COOK TIME 4 MINS

» **Makes 2 drinks**

¾ cup gin

3 slices (⅛ inch thick) fresh ginger

¼ cup agave or another liquid sweetener you like

¼ cup orange juice

Juice of 1 lime

½ cup ginger beer or ginger ale

2 sprigs fresh mint, for garnish

MALHOTRA MUDDLE

Pour the gin into a jar with a tight-fitting lid and add the ginger. Use the back of a spoon and mash the fuck outta the ginger. Add the agave, orange juice, and lime juice. Fill the jar with ice and shake the hell out of it until everything is mashed up and chilled. Pour that into 2 ice-filled cocktail glasses, straining out the mashed-up ginger. Top with the ginger beer or ginger ale and garnish with mint to class that shit up.

DID YOU KNOW?

Originally called "corpse crop," wheatgrass used to be harvested from cemeteries. Would you like that free sample shot of wheatgrass juice now?

Michelle's friend Myra is one of the kindest girls around. But if you mess with her, she won't hesitate to put you in your fucking place. We made this drink to honor both her sweetness and her stealth badassery. Cheers, bitch. Miss you.

MYRAJITO

Splitting the ingredients between 2 tall glasses, stir together the lemon juice and sugar until the sugar starts to dissolve. Add ½ cup crushed ice to each glass then tear up the basil and mint leaves as you add them to the glasses. Smash that shit around, breaking up some of the basil to get that dope flavor, about 15 seconds. Then add the rum, the remaining crushed ice, and club soda. Stir, then serve right away.

COOK
TIME
3
MINS

>> **Makes 2 drinks or 1 for someone who's had a long-ass day**

¼ cup lemon juice
4 teaspoons sugar
2 cups crushed ice
14 fresh basil leaves
6 fresh mint leaves
½ cup white rum
¾ cup club soda

SHOTS
SHOTS
SHOTS
SINCE 2012

COOK TIME 10 MINS

>> **Makes 4 cups**

MIX

½ cup semisweet chocolate chips

3 tablespoons unsweetened cocoa powder*

2 teaspoons arrowroot powder or cornstarch

¼ teaspoon ground cinnamon

2 teaspoons sugar (optional)**

HOT CHOCOLATE

4 cups nondairy milk***

Toppings: whipped cream (page 192), candy cane bits, marshmallows

It's on the baking aisle kinda near the flour, we swear.

***There's already sugar in this from the chocolate chips, but if you know you like it sweet, add this in.*

****We used almond but whateverthefuck you've got will work.*

Honestly this recipe made it in the book just so we could take a photo of the quilt Matt's grandmother made for him. Thanks for the quilt, Grandma! It's part of the US Library of fucking Congress now.

HOT CHOCOLATE MIX

1 To make the mix: Throw the chocolate chips, cocoa powder, arrowroot powder, cinnamon, and sugar (if you're using it) into a blender or food processor and let that shit run until everything is a fine powder. You can store this away in the pantry or get right to making some hot chocolate.

2 To make hot chocolate: Warm up the milk in a saucepan over medium-low heat until small bubbles start to form at the edge of the pan. Whisk in the mix until there are no clumps and keep stirring it for 1½ to 2 minutes. You never want this shit to start simmering, just little bubbles around the edges. Serve right away with whipped cream, candy cane bits, marshmallows, whateverthefuck you're into.

ROADSIDE ASSISTANCE

Double or quadruple this recipe to keep this hot shit handy whenever you want to warm up with something sweet. Hot chocolate for one? We've got your lonely ass covered. Just use 2 tablespoons of the mix for every cup of milk you want to use.

THIS SHIT IS LIKE A HUG FOR YOUR SOUL

Michelle's friend Amber looks like a fucking cartoon deer and is straight-up hilarious once you get to know her. Wanna think you're as funny as Amber? Drink 4 of these.

AMBER WAVES

Combine the bourbon, lemon juice, and maple syrup in a glass. Pour into 2 ice-filled glasses. Add the ginger beer on top of each glass and top with a twist of lemon or some fancy shit like that. Serve right away.

COOK TIME 3 MINS

>> **Makes 2 drinks**

¾ cup bourbon

¼ cup lemon juice

¼ cup pure maple syrup

1 cup ginger beer or ginger ale

THUG KITCHEN Brewing

COOK TIME 3 MINS

>> **Makes 2 drinks**

2 cups ginger ale or ginger beer

½ cup fresh tangerine juice*

¾ cup bourbon

Whether you're a salty sailor or just enjoy cursing like one, you're getting more than two-thirds of your DV of vitamin C in this sparkly son of a bitch. FUCK SCURVY. Yell it loud. Frighten the neighbors.

GINGER FIZZ

Mix all this shit together in a big glass then split it between 2 ice-filled cups. Throw in a sliced piece of the tangerine peel if you wanna look fancy, then drink up.

* This took about 6 tangerines, but you can use whatever oranges look legit at your store. Blood oranges, mandarins, sumos, regular oranges, whatever is good.

Growing up, Matt had a neighbor who was a single mom of two boys. When she wasn't juggling their school or sports schedules or feeding the neighborhood kids, she was walking through the house with a glass of wine and a power drill, fixing shit. Susan was one of the hardest-working women Matt knew and this drink is for her to finally take a load off. Respect.

LAZY SUSAN

Throw the berries, sugar, zest, and orange juice into a blender and run that shit until the berries are all blended up. Pour all that into a large pitcher through a fine-mesh sieve to catch any seeds from the berries. Stir in the rosé and sparkling water and serve over ice with some sliced citrus thrown in the glass if you wanna show off.

COOK TIME 5 MINS

>> **Makes enough for 4 people**

2 cups raspberries or strawberries, whatever looks better at the store

½ cup sugar

Grated zest of 1 lemon

Grated zest of 1 lime

1 cup orange juice

1 bottle (750ml) sparkling rosé wine

2 cups sparkling water

COOK TIME 3 MINS

>> **Makes enough for 4 people**

1 cup white rum

1 cup pineapple juice

1 cup frozen cherries

1 tablespoon lime juice

1 cup sparkling water or club soda

Don't let the name fool you, this is a classic rum cocktail, no gin in sight. Named after one of our favorite couples, the Jindras, this tropical treat will never let you down, just like them.

CHERRY JINDRA

In a blender, throw together the rum, pineapple juice, cherries, and lime juice and let that fucker rip until the cherries are all blended up. Stir in the sparkling water. Fill 4 tall glasses with crushed ice and pour in the good time.

DID YOU KNOW?

Nearly all frozen fruits and vegetables are grown and harvested in the Arctic to ensure peak flavor in every bag.

CALL IT A NIGHT

COOKIES, CAKES, AND OTHER SWEETS

FOOD EXITS

BROWN SUGAR BLUEBERRY POLENTA SCONES	158
SNICKERDOODLES	161
ALMOND CAKE WITH PEACH CARAMEL	162
BANANA CHOCOLATE CHIP COOKIES	165
CREAMSICLES	166
WINE CAKE	167
JASMINE RICE PUDDING	171
TAHINI FUDGE	172
NANA'S CHOCOLATE CRUNCH NO-BAKE COOKIES	174
COCONUT PRALINES	177
PUPPY CHOW	178
CINNAMON KETTLE CORN	179

40 MPH

>> **Makes about 8 scones**

1½ cups whole wheat pastry or all-purpose flour

1 cup cornmeal*

⅓ cup packed brown sugar, plus more for sprinkling

1 tablespoon baking powder

½ teaspoon ground cinnamon

¼ teaspoon salt

1 cup unsweetened plain almond milk, plus more for brushing

¼ cup olive oil

2 teaspoons vanilla extract

¾ cup blueberries, fresh (or still frozen is cool)

Like the finely ground kind you use to make cornbread. We used blue cornmeal, but that shit was just for looks. Use whateverthefuck you can find.

Crumbly and sweet, these scones are a legit way to start your day. Only the realest motherfuckers wake and bake.

BROWN SUGAR BLUEBERRY POLENTA SCONES

1 Crank your oven to 425°F. Line a baking sheet with parchment paper or foil.

2 Mix together the flour, cornmeal, brown sugar, baking powder, cinnamon, and salt in a large bowl. Whisk together the milk, oil, and vanilla in a medium glass. Not complicated.

3 Make a well in the center of the flour and pour in the milk mixture. Mix it together until it's almost all the way combined, but stop short. You don't want these perfectly blended just yet. Fold in the berries and mix until they're all in there but be careful not to overdo it because if you overmix they'll start getting gummy. This is one instance where it's okay to give a half-ass effort.

4 Plop the dough out on a cutting board and kinda press it into a rectangle about 1½ inches thick and 8 inches long. Halve lengthwise and then crosswise into 2-inch-wide scones. Throw them on the baking sheet and brush them with some almond milk and sprinkle with sugar.

5 Bake until they look a little golden on the bottom, 12 to 15 minutes. Let them cool on a wire rack for 5 to 10 minutes before serving so you don't burn the fuck out of your tongue on a molten-hot berry. Been there. They are best served the day they're made because they'll get soft the longer they're left out.

WHEN YOU'RE TRYING TO START BEEF AT THE UPCOMING BAKE SALE

We dunno what the fuck snickerdoodle actually means. Sounds like some kind of designer dog. People just got lazy and made a gibberish word, that's chill.

SNICKERDOODLES

1 Crank up your oven to 400°F. Set out a baking sheet.

2 Add the olive oil, coconut oil, 1 cup of the sugar, and the almond milk to a food processor and run that motherfucker until everything is all creamed up together. Add the flour, cream of tartar, baking soda, and salt, then pulse until the dough comes together. If your dough still looks a little dry, just add more almond milk 1 tablespoon at a time until that fucker starts acting right.

3 On a small plate, mix together the remaining 2 tablespoons sugar and the cinnamon and set aside.

4 Dump the dough out on the counter and start making balls about the size of a golf ball. Roll them around in the cinnamon mixture and then put them on the baking sheet. Gently press them down a little with a fork so that they look artisan and shit.

5 Bake until the bottoms look all golden, 8 to 10 minutes. Let them cool for at least 5 minutes before you dive in.

* This might seem like a fuckton of sugar, but it's half of what you'd find in a traditional recipe. So chill.

** It's an acidic powder that's a by-product of winemaking. It's an old-school ingredient you'll find with the spices or next to the baking shit at the store. It gives the cookies their classic taste, so don't skip it.

COOK TIME 15 MINS

>> **Makes 24 but that really depends on how fucking big you want your cookies**

½ cup olive oil

¼ cup coconut oil

1 cup plus 2 tablespoons sugar*

⅓ cup almond milk

2 cups whole wheat pastry flour or all-purpose flour

2 teaspoons cream of tartar**

1 teaspoon baking soda

¼ teaspoon salt

2 teaspoons ground cinnamon

COOK
TIME
40
MINS

>> **Makes 1 cake, enough for 1 to 10 people**

CAKE

1 cup unsweetened plain almond milk

1 teaspoon apple cider vinegar

1¾ cups whole wheat pastry flour, all-purpose flour, or a mix*

½ teaspoon salt

1 teaspoon baking powder

⅔ cup sugar

⅓ cup olive oil

2 teaspoons almond extract

1 teaspoon vanilla extract

PEACH CARAMEL

2 ripe peaches, pitted and cut into wedges (about 3 cups)

1 tablespoon lemon juice

½ cup water

1 tablespoon vanilla extract

1 cup sugar

Pinch of salt

Are you a terrible baker but wanna dazzle some motherfuckers with dessert? You've flipped to the right page. Welcome to "that one dessert you do really well" from this day forward.

ALMOND CAKE WITH PEACH CARAMEL

1 Warm the oven to 350°F. Grease and flour an 8-inch round cake pan.

2 Mix the almond milk and vinegar together in a glass.

3 In a medium bowl, whisk together the flour, salt, and baking powder. In a small bowl, whisk together the sugar, oil, extracts, and almond milk mixture. Make a crater in your dry ingredients and pour in the wet stuff. Stir that shit until it's just combined, a couple lumps are cool. Pour into the pan and bake until it looks kinda golden, 25 to 30 minutes. Let it cool in the pan for 10 minutes, then on a plate for at least 30 minutes before glazing with the caramel.

4 While the cake is baking, throw together the caramel: Throw the peaches and lemon juice into a blender or food processor and let that rip until it's smooth and liquidy in there. Gotta shitty blender? Add water, 1 tablespoon at a time, to get it going and use riper fruit next time, dumbass.

5 In a medium saucepan, combine the ½ cup water, vanilla, sugar, and salt and bring to a gentle boil over medium heat. Cook, stirring occasionally, until the mixture starts looking the color of maple syrup, about 10 minutes. Slowly whisk in the peach puree and continue stirring until all the sugar has dissolved, just another minute or two. Remove from the heat and let cool to room temperature.

6 When both the cake and caramel are cool, cut the cake into wedges and drizzle each piece with some caramel.

* You can replace three-quarters of the flour with almond meal (just ground-up almonds that kinda look like flour) if you wanna really turn this shit out.

ROADSIDE ASSISTANCE Top with some coconut Whipped Cream (page 192) if you wanna watch people lose their goddamn minds.

One bite of these cookies and you'll get taken back to your childhood when shit was simple and you didn't know what calories even meant.

BANANA CHOCOLATE CHIP COOKIES

1 Heat your oven to 350°F. Grab a baking sheet.

2 Whisk together the flour, baking powder, baking soda, and salt in a medium bowl. In a large bowl, mix together the sugars, banana puree, oil, and vanilla. Mix the flour into the wet mixture and stir until almost all the dry spots are gone. Fold in the chocolate until it's mixed in like a motherfucker. (If you got some time, these cookies taste even better if you can stick the dough covered in the fridge for at least 30 minutes and for up to 2 days.)

3 Scoop out a spoonful of dough about the size of a golf ball, place on the baking sheet, and sorta flatten the top a little with the back of your spoon. Keep going until you run out of dough. Bake until the bottoms are nice and golden, 12 to 15 minutes.

4 Let the cookies cool on a wire rack for at least 10 minutes before serving. PRACTICE SOME FUCKING WILLPOWER.

* Just throw 2 ripe bananas in a food processor or blender and run that until they're all smooth. You can use a potato masher and bowl too if you want a workout. Fuck, you could even use some banana baby food if you've got that lying around. Pumpkin or even mango would be chill too.

** We like this because it makes them look more bougie, but you can use 1 cup semisweet chocolate chips if that's easier.

COOK TIME 20 MINS

》 **Makes about 18 cookies depending on how you size them**

2¼ cups whole wheat pastry or all-purpose flour

1 teaspoon baking powder

½ teaspoon baking soda

½ teaspoon salt

½ cup sugar

½ cup packed brown sugar

⅔ cup banana puree*

⅓ cup safflower or olive oil

1 teaspoon vanilla extract

¾ cup chopped dark chocolate**

COOK TIME
3 MINS

>> **Makes about 4½ cups, enough for 10 pops (but that shit varies based on your molds, so halve the recipe if your molds are small)**

3 cups chopped and seeded orange segments

4 ripe bananas

1 cup unsweetened plain almond milk

1½ cups nondairy yogurt*

3 tablespoons pure maple syrup or agave

2 teaspoons vanilla extract

Make these when you want all of that childhood nostalgia without any of the weird artificial dye.

CREAMSICLES

1 Throw everything into a blender and give it a goddamn whirl until there are no chunks of banana or oranges left in there and everything looks smooth.

2 Pour this into your molds and stick in the freezer for about 40 minutes. After 40 minutes, take out your pop molds and then push the pop sticks in. Freezing these fuckers a little bit first helps make sure you won't push the stick all the way through and end up with icy skewers. Learn from our messy-ass mistakes. Freeze until completely frozen. Yeah, we have to say that shit because people are impatient.

3 Kick back with one whenever life gets too hot to handle. They will keep for at least a month in the freezer.

* We used almond yogurt, but use whatever you can find like coconut or soy. Just get plain or vanilla. None of that blueberry and banana bullshit; use some damn sense.

There's rum cake and that's pretty dope, right? So why not wine? Some people might see a cake and ask why, we see a cake and ask wine.

WINE CAKE

1 Warm up the oven to 350°F. Grease and flour a standard Bundt pan.

2 Make the cake: In a large bowl, whisk together the sugar, oil, coconut milk, wine, and vanilla. In a medium bowl, whisk together the flour, baking powder, baking soda, cinnamon, nutmeg, and salt. Gently stir the dry mixture into the wet, then mix that shit up until there aren't any more huge dry spots. Don't overmix this though, just chill.

3 Pour the batter into the prepared pan and bake until a toothpick stuck into it comes out clean, 35 to 45 minutes. Let it cool in the pan for 10 minutes, then stick a plate on top of that motherfucker and flip it over to get it out of the pan and onto the plate to cool.

4 Once the cake has cooled, you can add the glaze. Whisk together the powdered sugar, wine, lemon juice, and vanilla until there aren't any clumps. Drizzle over the cooled cake and slice that sweet son of a bitch up.

ROADSIDE ASSISTANCE Feeling lazy? Skip the glazing step and just dust it with some powdered sugar and serve it with fruit or Whipped Cream (page 192). DONE.

COOK TIME 50 MINS

>> **Makes 1 dope-ass cake, so enough for like . . . 1 cake's worth of people**

CAKE

1 cup sugar

¼ cup olive oil

1 can (14 ounces) coconut milk

¾ cup dry white wine

1 tablespoon vanilla extract

3½ cups whole wheat pastry flour or all-purpose flour

2 teaspoons baking powder

1 teaspoon baking soda

1½ teaspoons ground cinnamon

1 teaspoon ground nutmeg

½ teaspoon salt

SWEET SUGAR GLAZE

1¼ cups powdered sugar

¼ cup wine (whatever you used for the cake)

2 teaspoons lemon juice

1 teaspoon vanilla extract

1 **Wine Cake** (page 167)
2 **Sweet Sugar Glaze**
3 **Wine**
4 **Couple of assholes**

EAT FLOWERS
KICK ASS

Nothing makes you feel like more of a fucking boss than eating flowers. This dessert lets you snack like you're royalty but it's really just some dressed-up rice from the market. It's cheap as hell to make, but nobody will notice. FLOWER POWER, BITCHES.

JASMINE RICE PUDDING

1 Warm the coconut oil in a large soup pot over medium heat. Add the rice and stir until it smells kinda toasted, then add the sugar. Slowly start adding 8 cups of the milk, 2 cups at a time (so that you don't splash that shit all over yourself), along with the tea bags and salt. Set the remaining 1 cup milk aside for later.

2 Bring that shit to a simmer, stirring frequently, until the rice is soft but not all mushy, 20 to 30 minutes. Remove from the heat, remove the tea bags, pour the reserved 1 cup almond milk in, then stick that shit in the fridge to chill. (You can eat it warm if you really want but we think it's best served cold.)

3 Serve chilled and topped up with whateverthefuck you're into.

COOK TIME 30 MINS

>> **Makes enough for 4 to 6 people**

2 tablespoons coconut oil

1½ cups jasmine rice, rinsed

¼ cup sugar

9 cups unsweetened plain almond milk, warmed

8 jasmine tea bags

¼ teaspoon salt

Toppings: jasmine petals, mint, toasted almonds, toasted coconut, fresh berries

>> **Makes enough for 4 to 6 people**

1 cup canned coconut milk

1 cup tahini*

½ cup powdered sugar

¼ cup coconut oil

4–5 dates, pitted

¼ teaspoon salt

¼ cup chopped pistachios**

Yes, you're reading that correctly. Yes, it tastes fucking amazing. No, we won't just make it for you and send you some.

TAHINI FUDGE

1 Grab an 8-inch square baking dish and grease it up.

2 Throw the coconut milk, tahini, powdered sugar, oil, dates, and salt all together in a blender and let that shit run until it looks all smooth inside.

3 Pour into the baking dish, sprinkle with the pistachios, and refrigerate for at least 1 hour before cutting and serving.

* WTF? See page 189.

** Pistachios look dope as fuck and taste great, but if you're trying to save some cash any kind of chopped nuts would work.

CAN'T SPELL FUDGE
WITHOUT F-U

>> **Makes about
24 cookies**

**2 cups semisweet
chocolate chips**

**½ cup chunky low-salt
peanut butter**

**2½ cups broken-up
saltine crackers***

** You want the broken-up
pieces no bigger than a
quarter. Also check the
ingredient list when
you're buying your
crackers and try to buy
ones that don't have a
bunch of garbage in them.*

Tired of eating raw cookie dough? Scared to turn
on the oven? As always, Nana's got your back.

NANA'S CHOCOLATE CRUNCH NO-BAKE COOKIES

I Line a rimmed baking sheet with some parchment or wax
paper.

2 Melt the chocolate chips in a double boiler or the microwave
(see page 191). Add the peanut butter to the chocolate chips and
stir until everything is melted and mixed together. Remove from
the heat.

3 Add the saltines and stir that shit up until there's no more dry
clumps. This might take a little longer than you think it should,
but just keep stirring. This shit is almost over.

4 Once everything is coated, grab a big spoon and dollop piles of
the chocolate saltine mixture about the size of an egg onto the
lined baking sheet. Then put the baking sheet in a cool area to
let the chocolate harden up before diving in, 15 to 45 minutes
depending on the temperature in your place. So maybe don't try
this shit on a hot summer day. You can stick this in the fridge if
you're in a rush and have the space.

THEY TASTE A LOT BETTER
THAN THEY LOOK

You ever get the craving for caramel in cookie form? Well that's exactly what these little fuckers are, but pace yourself because these are sweet as shit. One goes a long way.

COCONUT PRALINES

COOK TIME 15 MINS

>> **Makes about 12 pralines**

1 cup sugar

½ cup packed brown sugar

¼ cup coconut milk or unsweetened plain almond milk

¼ cup coconut oil

½ teaspoon baking soda

⅛ teaspoon salt

1½ cups chopped pecans

1½ teaspoons vanilla extract

1 Line a large baking sheet with wax paper and set aside.

2 Combine the sugars, milk, oil, and baking soda in a medium saucepan. Bring to a simmer over medium heat, stirring constantly, about 5 minutes. Let it stay just under boiling, stirring, until there seem to be bubbles all through it but you start to hear the sugar granules kinda scrape along the bottom of the pot, 3 to 5 minutes.

3 Remove the pan from the heat, add the pecans and vanilla, and keep stirring that shit until you feel it start to thicken up, about a minute. Working kinda quick, you need to drop cookie-size spoonfuls of the mix onto the baking sheet to form piles about 2 inches wide. Let them cool and harden completely, about 30 minutes. You can let them cool in the fridge if you've got the space.

4 Serve right away, or store the pralines in an airtight container at room temperature for 2 to 3 days.

COOK TIME 15 MINS

>> **Makes 6 cups, or enough for 1 sleepover**

6 cups square, waffle-cut cereal, such as Chex*

1½ cups semisweet chocolate chips

¾ cup chunky almond or peanut butter

1½ cups powdered sugar**

You can do half rice Chex, half corn, some wheat, whateverthefuck you like or is on sale.

*** What'd you expect? THIS IS A GODDAMN DESSERT.*

WHAT THE FUCK YOU MEAN you've never heard of puppy chow!? No, it's not fucking dog food. It's the single greatest dessert you could ever make as a kid with limited baking skills. This is like the LEGOs of desserts because anyone between 2 and 99 is gonna love this shit.

PUPPY CHOW

1 Pour the cereal into a large heatproof bowl and set that shit aside.

2 In a double boiler, homemade fake out, or microwave, melt the chocolate chips and the almond butter together until they are all mixed up and the chips have all melted. Already confused? See page 191.

3 While the chocolate is melting, measure out the powdered sugar and dump it in the largest plastic bag you've got. Growing up we used to do this shit in a garbage bag but looking back that's kinda gross so we don't recommend it.

4 When the chocolate is melted, pour it all over the cereal and stir until every piece looks mostly coated. Dump the chocolate-covered cereal into the sugar bag, twist it closed, and shake the shit out of it so that all the cereal gets sugar on it. DON'T ACCIDENTLY LET THE BAG OPEN. That'd make a goddamn mess and you'd hafta just move out instead of cleaning it up.

5 Pour this into a big bowl and serve immediately or stick it in an airtight container for later. Lasts about 4 days but there's no fucking way it doesn't get eaten in 4 hours.

We've all got that metal tin at home that once was filled with delicious different flavors of popcorn, but now that shit is probably filled with sewing supplies. Cook up this cinnamon snack and reclaim that tin for its rightful purpose.

CINNAMON KETTLE CORN

COOK TIME 7 MINS

>> **Makes about 6 cups**

3 tablespoons refined coconut oil

½ cup popcorn kernels

3 tablespoons sugar

½ teaspoon ground cinnamon

⅛ teaspoon cayenne pepper

¼ teaspoon salt

1 In a large heavy pot, heat the oil over medium heat. Add a couple of kernels of popcorn, put on the lid, and shake it around every now and then. Once one of them pops that means your pan is ready. This might take up to 1½ minutes.

2 When the pan is hot, add the rest of the kernels and the sugar and cover that fucker up with a lid. If you have a glass lid, use that so you can supervise the corn. Shake the pan around every couple of seconds so those bitches don't burn. It's like stirring without releasing all the heat. If they don't start popping within the first 30 seconds, turn your heat up just a lil bit. Soon it should start to sound like motherfucking firecrackers. Once you hear more than a couple seconds between pops, remove from the heat. See, that took no fucking time at all.

3 Pour the popcorn into a big-ass bowl. Sprinkle in the cinnamon, cayenne, and salt and toss it around so everything gets coated. Taste and add more of whatever if that is your thing. This keeps for a couple days in an airtight container if you've got strong self-control.

DRIVER'S ED

If any of this shit looks familiar, that's because we've covered some of this in our other books. Obviously, you own this book, but we can't just fucking assume you have the other ones. If you do, you have great taste. But for those who don't, we're gonna give you a quick rundown on some Thug Kitchen basics so you can upgrade whatever skills you've got now.

BASIC POT OF BEANS

If you're new to this, you might notice lots of our recipes call for beans. There's no shame using canned, but throwing together a pot of beans is probably some of the simplest shit you can do in the kitchen. You just gotta plan ahead and stay chill. The steps are the same regardless of what bean you're using; only the cooking times change. Here's some guidelines, but trust your taste. The beans are done when at least five of them taste tender and are cooked through. Don't just trust one bean, one bean can lie and fuck everything up. So remember to sample multiple beans. Keep simmering until you get there. Easy shit.

First, pick through the dried beans and throw out any that look fucked up, then rinse the winners. Put them in a big container and cover with a couple inches of water. They're going to swell up as they soak and you don't want those beany bastards sticking outta the water. Soak them overnight or for at least 4 hours. This will help cut down on your cook time. Throw them in the water before you leave for work and they're ready to cook when you get home.

When you're ready to cook the beans, drain off the soaking water then throw the beans in a pot. Add a bunch of fresh water to the pot, about three times the height of the beans in the pot. Simmer that shit, uncovered, until the beans are tender. Add a couple pinches of salt in the last 10 minutes of cooking for flavor. Drain away any extra liquid in the pot and store the cooked beans in the fridge or freezer until you're ready to use them. No can opener required.

Here are some bean basics, but remember that shit changes depending on how long you soaked your beans and how old they are. If you picked up some lentils or split peas, congrats, because you don't need to soak those fuckers at all. Just follow the directions above and you're in business. Beans and lentils tend to triple in size when you cook them, so if you want to end up with about 1½ cups of cooked beans (the standard can measurement), you want to start with ½ cup dried beans.

STANDARD COOKING TIMES

» **Black beans:** 1 to 1½ hours

» **Black-eyed peas:** 1 hour

» **Garbanzo beans/ chickpeas (same shit):** 1½ hours

» **Kidney and cannellini beans:** 1½ hours

» **White, Great Northern, and navy beans:** 1 to 1½ hours

» **Pinto beans:** 1½ to 2 hours

» **Yellow or green split peas:** 30 to 40 minutes

» **Green or brown lentils:** 20 to 35 minutes

GRAINS

Cooking grains tends to go quicker than cooking beans, but these motherfuckers require a little more maintenance. Just like beans, know that they're gonna double in volume when you cook 'em, so 1 cup of uncooked rice will give you 2 cups cooked. Use the following guides to get some grains going, just be sure to adjust that shit for how much you need for whatever you're making. If you ever end up with extra water in the pot when your grains are done, just drain that shit off. You don't wanna cook the grains until they are all mushy. Also, if you run out of water and your grains aren't done, just pour more in. You're not gonna fuck anything up. You got this. FUCKING BELIEVE IN YOURSELF. WE BELIEVE IN YOU AND WE'VE NEVER EVEN MET.

BROWN RICE

You might think this is some hippie health food, but it packs way more nutrition and flavor on the table than white rice. We've always got a big pot of cooked brown rice in the fridge, and your ass should too. Shit, you could even freeze it into whatever portions you like and heat it up as you need it. If you're still feeling skeptical, try out the short-grain variety (below). That nutty, delicious son of a bitch will make you forget white rice altogether. You can cook the long-grain variety in the same way, but that shit is gonna take about 15 minutes longer and an extra ½ cup water.

BASIC POT OF BROWN RICE

Makes about 4 cups

1 teaspoon olive or coconut oil (optional)*

2 cups short-grain brown rice

Pinch of salt

3½ cups water

This oil business is optional, but it gives the rice a nuttier taste. Your call, champ.

1 In a medium saucepan, heat the oil (if using) over medium heat. Add the rice and sauté that shit until it smells a little nutty, about 2 minutes. Add the salt and water and stir. Bring to a simmer, then reduce the heat, cover, and let this very softly simmer until all the water is absorbed and the rice is tender, about 35 minutes.

2 Did you fuck up the heat and the rice is tender but there's still water? Just drain that shit. Is the rice not done but all the water is gone? Just stir in a little more water, reduce the heat, and keep going. Don't let some tiny-ass rice get you off your game. YOU. GOT. THIS.

BARLEY

This grain is nutty, chewy, and highly underrated. Not only is it full of fiber but it's packed with selenium, copper, and manganese, so you know you're getting your money's worth. There are two kinds of barley you're gonna run into at the store: hulled and pearled. Hulled takes longer to cook but has more fiber and other good shit than the pearled variety, which has that stuff polished off. Pearled barley is super creamy and easier to find in most stores, so just use what you've got. For hulled barley, add 1 cup of the grain to 3 cups of water on the stove with a pinch of salt. Bring it to a boil, then simmer that shit with a lid on it until it's tender, 40 to 50 minutes. For pearled, keep the grain-to-water ratio the same, but simmer it uncovered until it's tender, about 25 minutes. Want it less creamy? Just rinse that shit when it's done cooking.

COUSCOUS

This cooks quickly since technically it's a pasta, not a grain. Don't believe us? Look that shit up. These mini motherfuckers will be ready in 10 minutes flat. Throw 1 cup couscous in a pot or bowl with a lid and a pinch of salt. Add 1¼ cups boiling water, stir, and throw that lid on. No heat under the pot or nothing. Just let that sit for 8 minutes, then fluff the couscous with a fork and serve. Fucking done.

MILLET

Yeah, this kinda looks like birdseed, but it's cheap as fuck and deserves more love in the kitchen. It's like a mix between quinoa and brown rice and worthy of a test run on your plate. Throw 1 cup of millet in a medium pot over medium heat and sauté it around until it smells toasty, about 2 minutes. Add 2 cups water and a pinch of salt and simmer that shit, covered, until the millet is tender, 25 to 35 minutes.

QUINOA

Some people cook this protein-packed grain like rice but treat it like pasta. To cook, bring 2 cups water to boil in a medium pot with a pinch of salt, drop in ½ cup quinoa and simmer, uncovered, until the quinoa is tender, 15 to 20 minutes. Drain away any water that's left.

PLANKS

CHOPPED

STICKS

HALF-
MOONS

CONFUSED ON HOW SHIT SHOULD LOOK WHEN WE TELL YOU HOW TO CUT IT A SPECIFIC WAY?

Use this page as your quick reference guide
to figure out what we're talking about.

MATCHSTICKS

QUARTER-
MOONS

RIBBONS WITH
VEGGIE GRATER

SHREDDED

THE SKINNY ON FAT

When it comes to cooking and baking, not all oils are created equal or work for every job. Here's a quick rundown on what to use and where to use it. No matter what you pick, start cooking once the oils start to shimmer. If your shit starts smoking, turn down the heat or use another oil because you already messed up. You have to pick an oil that's right for the job. Use the chart below to figure it out.

AVOID

Right out the gate, DO NOT go buying some bullshit like these

» **Vegetable oil**

» **Vegetable shortening**
   (particularly if it is full of partially hydrogenated oils)

» **Canola oil**

   Most of these oils are highly refined and offer no nutritional trade-off. Grab something else and get your money's worth.

LOW TO MEDIUM HEAT

» **Olive oil**

» **Unrefined coconut oil**
   (this one tastes like coconut, stable at room temp)

» **Any of the high-heat oils**
   (see above right)

HIGH HEAT

» **Refined coconut oil**
   (no coconut taste, stable at room temp)

» **Safflower oil**

» **Grapeseed oil**

» **Peanut oil**

OILS FOR DRIZZLING, DRESSINGS, AND EXTRA FLAVOR

» **Extra virgin olive oil**

» **Toasted sesame oil**

BASIC SHIT TO ROAST AT HOME

Stop buying roasted bell peppers and garlic at the store because honestly you're just roasting your goddamn money. And if you're buying canned beets, you must hate yourself because they taste like dirt and batteries. Take 2 seconds to figure out how to do this on your own and you'll never look back. This shit's so easy to do and will save you cash. So grab some foil and get to roasting.

BEETS

Crank the oven to 400°F. Slice all the leaves and shit off the top of the beets, scrub them clean, but leave the skin on. Try to grab beets of the same size so they all roast at the same speed. Wrap them in foil all together in a group, then stick those blood-red bastards in the oven (use a baking sheet in case they leak a little). Roast them until you can stick a fork in them with no resistance, 45 minutes to 1 hour.

When the beets have chilled for a bit, you can peel them. Hold one in a paper towel and use the paper towel to kinda rub the skin off. If you cooked those bitches long enough this should be super easy. You can store them in the fridge for up to a week, so you can throw them into a salad or bowl whenever, or use them up right now. Whatever.

If you like to eat beets on the regular, then don't stress about roasting them separately. Next time you're baking any savory dish at 375°F or higher for a while, just toss a foil packet of these fuckers in and let them bum a roast ride. Just keep an eye on them if the temperature is higher than 425°F because they can dry out. Just add a tablespoon of water to the packet when you check on them if that shit starts to happen.

BELL PEPPERS

METHOD I: GAS: You can do as many of these as you have burners on your stove but we usually stick to two so we don't get too distracted. Set aside a large piece of foil for each pepper you're roasting. Place a bell pepper directly on the burner of a gas stove and crank the heat to high. Burn the ever-living fuck outta the skin of the pepper, rotating it until every side is blackened. This should take 8 to 10 minutes for the whole pepper. Chill the fuck out, the more burnt it looks the better. When the pepper is blackened all the way around, place it in a piece of foil and wrap it up so that no steam can escape. It needs to cool down for at least 15 minutes, so go do something else and then come back. You can let this sit for a while longer if you need to, so move on if you're busy with other shit in the kitchen.

When the peppers have cooled you'll be able to peel the burnt skin off with your hands no problem. Cut off the top of the pepper where the stem is still attached and start pulling off all the burnt skin. Yeah, your hands might get a little dirty but just fucking deal with it. Don't run the pepper under the sink thinking you're saving time because you'll lose that roasted flavor you worked so hard for, so don't go and fuck things up now.

It's cool if you leave a couple charred pieces here and there, no need to be a perfectionist. Once the peppers are cleaned, chop off the tops, scrape out the guts and seeds, and then go make something badass. You can do this a day or two in advance, just keep 'em in the fridge.

METHOD 2: ELECTRIC: If you're working with an electric stove, we didn't forget about you but you do have our sympathies. Crank your oven to 400°F and line a baking sheet with some foil. Lay your peppers down on there, roast them for 25 minutes, turn, and roast them for 25 more until they look all charred and soft. Wrap them up in foil just like the gas stove directions and follow the rest of the steps to peel them. Done and fucking done.

GARLIC

Crank your oven to 400°F. Pull off all the extra layers of paper around a whole bulb of garlic. Slice the top ¼ inch right off the bulb of garlic to expose its innards. Put that shit on a piece of foil, pour ½ teaspoon of olive oil over the cut garlic top, then wrap the bulb up in the foil. Roast in the oven until all the cloves look all golden and smell goddamn delicious, about 40 minutes. You can do a bunch of bulbs at a time in the same foil pouch thing if you're all about that garlic life.

Let it cool for a bit and then squeeze out as many cloves as you need. It will keep for at least 2 weeks in the fridge.

Know you'll want roasted garlic in the future but don't want to heat the oven up? Just follow the directions for roasting alongside some other shit like we wrote opposite for the beets. Same rules apply.

WTF IS THAT?!

BRAGG LIQUID AMINOS

Yeah, more hippie shit. It tastes and looks a lot like soy sauce but has a little something extra that's hard to explain. Bragg's is fucking delicious though, and totally something you should keep on hand. You can find this sauce near the soy sauce or vinegars at most stores or again, on the goddamn Internet.

CHIPOTLES IN ADOBO

These smoked jalapeño peppers packed in sauce add a slow-cooked taste to even the fastest of meals. You'll almost never use the whole can at once, so freeze the rest of that shit and defrost when needed. When you chop the chipotles, cut them open and scrape out the seeds. If you prefer it hot, then keep some of the seeds in, but think of your butthole tomorrow as you make that call. They are sold in a tiny can or jar, usually near the salsa and beans at the store.

GARAM MASALA

Don't freak out. Garam masala is just a badass spice blend that is as popular as fuck. It has all kinds of shit like cinnamon and cardamom in it, and once you have it you'll use it on everything. You can find it with the spices at any well-stocked grocery store, on the Internet, or at any Indian grocer in your area. Totally worth the buy.

LIQUID SMOKE

This shit does exactly what you think it does: adds a smoky flavor to whateverthefuck you're cooking up. It's made by collecting the smoke from burning wood chips, letting that cool, and adding a little water to the mix. It adds a shit-ton of flavor but is easy to overdo, so go easy when you're measuring that shit out. Sure you can do this yourself if you are crazy about that DIY shit, but just buy a bottle and save yourself the work. It's near the BBQ sauce at the store, so stop thinking you can't find it. It's there.

MISO

Miso paste is made from fermented beans and grains and comes in a bunch of fucking flavors. Because it's fermented, it's full of probiotics and all the good shit that's great for your gut. Always add it last to soups or anything hot so you don't overheat it and kill all that good stuff. Always salty but sometimes sweet, miso is a great way to add depth of flavor to a meal that will make your guests think you're a fucking magician in the kitchen. You can find it in the fridge at a well-stocked store; if it's stored on the shelf, it ain't worth your time or your money.

NOOCH

Nutritional yeast, or nooch if you're cool like that, is some real throwback hippie shit. It's deactivated yeast sold in flakes that makes everything taste kinda cheesy. It's packed with B_{12}, folate, selenium, zinc, and protein. You can find it in bulk bins at some grocery stores, near the soy sauce in jars sometimes, and on the Internet. It's not the same thing as brewer's yeast, which you don't ever fucking need.

PANKO BREAD CRUMBS

There are regular bread crumbs and then there's panko. There's no fucking comparison. Panko is much lighter than traditional bread crumbs and is broken into large, coarse flakes rather than tiny-ass sand-looking pieces. The crumbs are used to coat all types of fried and baked shit because they stay crisper longer than most bread crumbs. You can grab a box of these fuckers somewhere near the soy sauce in your grocery store or near the rest of the bread crumbs.

TAHINI

This creamy deliciousness is just like peanut butter, except it's made from sesame seeds. Think you've never had it? If you've ever had hummus, then you're fucking wrong. Tahini is a crucial ingredient in any hummus worth eating, but it's also used in plenty of other tasty-as-hell ways all over the world. Grab it near the falafel mix at the store and keep it handy from now on.

TEMPEH

This shit is fucking delicious but doesn't sound that way outta the gate, we get it. It's a brick made of fermented soybeans and because it's fermented, sometimes it might look like it has some mold on it, but just fucking go with it. It adds a great texture and kinda nutty taste to whatever you're cooking up. One cup of tempeh has 30 goddamn grams of protein in it, so you have no excuses to not try it. You can find it in the fridge of a well-stocked grocery store and the Internet.

TOFU

Everybody knows what this is, but most people have no fucking clue how it's made or how to fucking cook it. Tofu is made from soy milk that has been curdled, the liquid drained away, and the remaining solids are molded into bricks. By itself it can be soft and have no fucking flavor, so think of it more as something that needs to be fucking seasoned rather than as an ingredient that's bringing any flavor to the table. One cup of tofu has 20 grams of protein, is rich in calcium and iron, and is cholesterol-free, so stop being afraid and try this fucker out at home. You can find it in the fridge packed in water and in aseptic containers near the soy sauce at the store.

PANTRY PRIMER

Here we piled together a list of simple shit you need to be able to cook like the true boss you are. We know it looks kinda long, but trust us, you'll use all of it if you're cooking like you should. This is basic grocery store shit so you shouldn't have to change up your shopping routine to find any of this stuff. Now make a list, get your ass to the store, and be nice as fuck to the cashier. They could probably use it. Unless you've bagged groceries to pay bills, you don't know the struggle.

BASIC DRIED HERBS AND SPICES

» One good, all-purpose, no-salt seasoning blend
» Basil
» Black pepper
» Cayenne pepper
» Celery seed
» Chili powder
» Cinnamon
» Cumin
» Garlic powder (granulated garlic is cool too)
» Onion powder
» Oregano
» Salt
» Smoked paprika
» Thyme
» Curry powder

PANTRY SHIT

» Olive oil
» A neutral-tasting oil (peanut, safflower, or grapeseed)
» Soy sauce, Bragg's aminos, or tamari
» A nut butter you prefer (peanut, almond, tahini, whatever)
» Rice vinegar
» One other vinegar you prefer (apple cider, balsamic, white wine, whateverthefuck you find)
» Your favorite grain (short-grain brown rice for the motherfucking win)
» Your favorite pasta noodles

» Canned no-salt-added diced tomatoes
» Your favorite dried and canned beans (Keep both stocked for when you're in a hurry and when you can take your time.)
» Your go-to flour (whole wheat pastry, all-purpose, rice, whatever your favorite shit is)

VEGETABLE BASICS

» Yellow and red onions
» Garlic
» Carrots
» Some kind of leafy green like cabbage, spinach, or kale
» Frozen green peas
» Lemons

If you're able to keep most of this at your place, you should always be able to make something to eat even if the fridge looks bare. Don't stress if you can't get this all at once because money is tight or whatever. It takes time to get your cabinet game on lock, so be patient with yourself and keep a running list of what you need on your cell phone. That will: (1) keep you from buying six things of cinnamon in 2 months (we've been there) and (2) help you make sure you're grabbing exactly what you need when shit goes on sale.

BASIC KITCHEN HOW TO'S

Here are some basic recipes for how to make real simple shit for your kitchen.

MELTING CHOCOLATE

There's a few places in this book (and in life if you're living right) where you need to melt some chocolate. If you do that shit too quickly or use too high a heat, you're gonna get a bowl of grainy, burnt mud. So follow our instructions and dessert will be right around the fucking corner.

METHOD 1, MICROWAVE: You can melt chocolate quickly and use the least amount of dishes by doing it this way. Slowly heat it in the microwave in 30-second increments, stirring in between, until it's completely melted. The total amount of time will depend on how much chocolate you're fucking with. Don't get crazy and try to do that shit in one big go because it'll get all messed up. We promise, we've been there. Just keeping stirring it every 30 seconds and heating it again until it's all melted and you're good to go.

METHOD 2, DOUBLE BOILER: No microwave? No problem. You get to build a DIY double boiler like a motherfucking boss. Grab a medium saucepan and fill it with 2 to 3 inches of water. Throw an all-metal bowl on top of that and be sure the whole mouth of the pan is covered and that the water inside isn't touching the bottom of the metal bowl. Put this over medium-low heat and add the chocolate to the bowl. The steam will melt the chocolate. Just keep stirring and trust the fucking method. When the chocolate looks all smooth, turn off the heat, and take the bowl off the pan. Obviously the bowl is gonna be hot as hell so be careful.

ZESTING CITRUS

If a recipe calls for zest, they want you to get all the flavorful essential oils from the outside rind of whatever citrus fruit they're asking about in the dish. There's two ways to do this shit:

METHOD 1, A GRATER: This is easiest but more likely to fuck up your knuckles if you're not careful. Grab your box grater or if you have a finer grater for nutmeg or Parmesan, use that. Using the smallest side of whatever grater you grabbed, gently scrape off the waxy outside colored layer of the citrus fruit. The white spongy layer (aka the pith if someone is trying to get fucking technical) is bitter and gross like your ex, so don't grate down past that. Keep going around the outside of the fruit until you get enough for your recipe.

METHOD 2, A KNIFE/VEGGIE PEELER: This way takes a sharp knife or veggie peeler and a steady hand, but we think you're ready. FUCK THAT, WE KNOW YOU'RE READY. Take your knife or peeler and shave off a thin-ass layer off the rind. Set that on your cutting board, cut it into crazy-thin strips, then dice those up so you get a minced-up zest. This method is awesome because you usually get more of the oils to stay in the skin where you need it, instead of all over your grater, so you get more bang in your zest, which is all any of us really wants. Life is all about banging with zest.

1 can (14 ounces)
coconut milk, chilled*

2 tablespoons
powdered sugar

½ teaspoon vanilla
extract (optional)

** Put that in the fridge the
night before so you know
it's cold enough. You
could do it an hour before
you make this, but you're
probably gonna forget.*

This whip is ready in no time flat, especially if you keep the coconut milk in the fridge, always waiting for your next snack attack. Throw it on some berries, throw it on a slice of Wine Cake (page 167), hell, even throw it on a nipple. Get weird.

WHIPPED CREAM

1 You need some electric beaters or a stand mixer to do this. It doesn't matter how much you lift bro, you're not strong enough to do this by hand. Trust us. Stick a bowl and the beaters in the freezer for 15 minutes to let that shit get frosty.

2 Take them out after 15 minutes and grab the milk from the fridge without shaking it up. Open up the can and scoop out all the thick white cream on the top half of the can and put it in the chilled bowl. (Leave that clearish liquid in the can and use it for a smoothie or something later. You're welcome.) Sift in the powdered sugar (so there aren't any chunks), then add the vanilla, if using.

3 Now beat the fuck out of it on medium-high until it starts looking all fluffy and whipped cream like, 1 to 2 minutes. Serve right away.

What the fuck happened that convinced us all that we can't do this shit ourselves? Can you brush your teeth? Then you can make this without relying on some steam-filled sabotage bag waiting to burn your face and your wallet.

POPPING YOUR OWN POPCORN

›› **Makes about 7 cups**

1½ tablespoons grapeseed or refined coconut oil

½ cup popcorn kernels

1 In a big-ass pot with a lid, heat the oil over medium heat. Add a couple kernels of the corn, cover, and shake it around every now and then. Once one of them pops that means you're ready. This could take up to 1½ minutes.

2 When the pan is ready, add the rest of the kernels and cover that shit. (If you have a glass lid, you can use it here to supervise the action.) If they don't start popping within the first 30 seconds, turn your heat up just a lil bit. Soon it should start to sound like motherfucking firecrackers are going off in your kitchen as all the kernels start exploding. Shake the pan around every couple of seconds to keep those bitches from burning. It's like stirring but without releasing any heat. You'll smell it if it's starting to burn, so don't overthink this. Once you hear more than 2 to 3 seconds between pops, remove from the heat. See? That took no time at all. Now you'll never go back to the bagged bullshit.

YES IT REALLY IS THAT FUCKING EASY

1½ cups unsweetened plain almond milk

1 teaspoon apple cider vinegar or lemon juice

2 cups oat flour*

2 cups whole wheat pastry flour or all-purpose flour

2 teaspoons baking soda

½ teaspoon salt

2 tablespoons olive oil

Calm the fuck down. Just grab 2 cups of rolled oats and run that shit in your food processor or blender until it looks like flour. Easy shit.

Soda bread? More like so damn easy. This recipe'll make you go from carb-less to carb-full in 45 minutes.

EASIER-THAN-PIE SODA BREAD

1 Crank up your oven to 400°F. And grease a loaf pan while you're at it.

2 In a large glass, mix together the milk and vinegar and set that aside for a sec.

3 In a large bowl, whisk together the flours, baking soda, and salt. Make a hole in the center of the flour and pour in the milk mixture and the oil. Stir that shit until you get some kind of a dough ball going. Looking too dry? Add a little splash of milk. Looking too fucking wet and goopy? Add another tablespoon or two of flour. Kinda knead it around with your hands to make sure it is all sticking together and then you are ready to bake that shit.

4 Form the dough into a loafish shape and stick it into the prepared pan. Brush the top with a little milk, then stick it in the oven and bake until the crust looks golden and the bread doesn't sound all doughy when you tap on it, 45 minutes to 1 hour. Let it cool for a bit in the pan, then take it out and let it cool until you're ready to slice that shit up.

You can whip up a salad in 5 fucking minutes any night of the week with a bottle of this in your fridge ready to go. It'll separate while you store it in the fridge, so just shake that shit real good before you use it. It will keep for a week or two, no problem.

EVERYDAY VINAIGRETTE

» Makes about 1½ cups

¼ cup diced shallot or sweet onion*

1 tablespoon Dijon mustard**

⅓ cup red wine vinegar

⅓ cup rice vinegar

½ cup olive oil

Pour all this together in a jar and shake the fuck out of it. Taste and add more of whatever you think it needs. You can switch out the vinegars with what you like to perfect your favorite combo. balsamic and Champagne? Sounds good. White wine and sherry vinegars? Fuck yeah. You do you. If you want to mix it up even more, add 2 teaspoons of your favorite dried herb or herb blend and shake that shit in.

* You can also sub in 2 cloves garlic if that's your style.

** Chill out, it won't taste like mustard. This just brings the whole dressing together. Trust.

1 clove garlic, minced

¼ cup minced parsley

⅓ cup balsamic vinegar

¼ cup olive oil

We like to serve this with some cut-up French or sourdough bread. It's key for when your squad wants to snack on shit but you only want to cook for 5 minutes and spend less than three bucks.

BALSAMIC HERB SAUCE

Mix everything together in a low, wide bowl. Serve right away or let it sit at room temperature, covered, for up to 1 hour ahead of time.

Warning: This recipe definitely contains peanuts. If you have a peanut allergy, move along. If you're still here, warning: This shit's delicious.

PEANUT SAUCE

In a medium glass, whisk together the water and peanut butter until it looks creamy. Add the vinegar, lime juice, ginger, soy sauce, maple syrup, and chili garlic paste and keep stirring until everything is incorporated. Stick that in the fridge until it's go time.

>> **Makes about 1¼ cups**

¼ cup warm water

⅓ cup creamy peanut butter

2 tablespoons seasoned rice vinegar

2 tablespoons lime juice

2 teaspoons minced fresh ginger

1 teaspoon soy sauce or tamari

1 teaspoon pure maple syrup or agave

1 teaspoon chili garlic paste

DID YOU KNOW?

Joshua trees actually prefer being called "Josh trees." They get kinda pissy when you say their full names.

⅓ cup tahini*

¼ cup warm water

2 tablespoons lemon juice

1 tablespoon seasoned rice vinegar

1 tablespoon olive oil

1 teaspoon soy sauce or tamari

1 clove garlic, minced

Want hummus but you're out of beans? Let this sauce come to the rescue. Pair it with baby carrots and celery and fight that snack attack in style.

TAHINI SAUCE

In a small glass, mix the tahini and warm water together until it's smooth and creamy. Stir in the lemon juice, vinegar, oil, soy sauce, and garlic. Serve right away or stick in the fridge until you're ready to fuck with it.

No clue? See page 189.

ROADSIDE ASSISTANCE

Wanna make it a salad dressing? Add another tablespoon of water and vinegar and 1 tablespoon toasted sesame oil and you're fucking good to go.

This simple sauce makes you sound like you know what the fuck you're doing in the kitchen.

CARAMELIZED ONION TOMATO SAUCE WITH THYME

Warm up the oil in a large skillet over medium-high heat. Add the onion and salt and sauté them around until the onions start to brown, about 8 minutes. Add the thyme and tomato paste and stir it up just enough that the tomato paste isn't in a giant blob in the pan. Add the canned tomatoes, then reduce the heat to medium. Let this shit all simmer around together, stirring occasionally, until the sauce starts to thicken up a little as the water from the tomatoes evaporates, 15 to 20 minutes. Use right away or stick it in the fridge or freezer for later.

» **Makes about 3 cups, enough for 4 people (or 1 pound of pasta, however you measure shit)**

2 tablespoons olive oil

1 medium yellow onion, sliced into thin strips

Pinch of salt

1 teaspoon dried thyme

1 tablespoon tomato paste

1 can (28 ounces) diced tomatoes with their juices

You ever eat tofu and the taste just makes you hate life? Most people can't cook tofu for shit, but this recipe is gonna fix that. This is gonna give you nice, crispy tofu without all the fucking oil. It's perfect to toss in a quick sauce, throw in a soup or pasta dish, or sneak in anywhere you want a little extra protein.

1 block extra-firm tofu,* drained and patted dry with some kind of towel

Pinch of salt

DRY-FRIED TOFU

1 Cut the tofu into planks about ¼-inch thick and then cut those planks in half widthwise. You should end up with around 20 square-ish pieces.

2 Warm up a large wok, cast-iron skillet, or skillet over medium-high heat. You wanna use something that's well seasoned here so that the tofu won't stick. Once the pan is hot, add the tofu in a single layer. You might have to do this in 2 batches depending on the size of your pan. The tofu should sizzle once it hits the pan so if that shit sounds quiet, turn the heat up a little.

3 Sprinkle the salt over the tofu and start gently pressing down on the tofu with your spatula. You'll hear the steam escape from under the tofu as you do this. It sounds kinda like high-pitched screams, but don't worry, the tofu was already dead when you bought it at the store. Don't try and flip it too early, you gotta let that shit get toasted. After 3 to 4 minutes, the bottom side should look golden brown. Flip it over and repeat. When the tofu is cooked all over you can then cut it into strips, triangles, or smaller squares, whateverthefuck you'd like in your food. It's just easier to keep that shit bigger for flipping purposes while you cook it.

WTF? See page 189.

All season, any reason, ready to rumble, tempeh crumble. Fold it into pasta, add it to a pizza, into a mess of greens, or into a scramble. Wherever it goes the flavor flows. Get into it.

ALL-SEASON TEMPEH CRUMBLE

1 Grab a large skillet or wok and warm up the olive oil over medium heat. Using your hands, crumble the tempeh into pieces no bigger than a nickel as you add them to the pan. Smaller is better than big chunks but there's really no wrong way to do this shit. Add the onion and sauté them together until the tempeh starts to brown, about 5 minutes.

2 Sprinkle the soy sauce all over everything in the pan and stir. Stir in the fennel seeds, basil, oregano, and thyme and sauté for 30 seconds. Fold in the lemon juice and garlic. Remove from the heat and shake in some red pepper flakes if you're into that.

* WTF? See page 189.

** WTF? See page 188.

ROADSIDE ASSISTANCE

Want it even simpler? Leave out the dried herbs. Wanna make it a side? Add 6 cups of chopped chard, kale, or spinach when you add the garlic and keep sautéing until that shit wilts down, about 2 minutes.

» **Makes about 3 cups**

2 teaspoons olive oil

1 block (8 ounces) tempeh*

1 yellow onion, chopped

1 tablespoon soy sauce or Bragg's**

2 teaspoons chopped fennel seeds

1 teaspoon dried basil

1 teaspoon dried oregano

1 teaspoon dried thyme

1 tablespoon lemon juice

3 cloves garlic, minced

Red pepper flakes (optional)

PESTO PRIMER

Pesto basically means any kind of sauce you've made from pounding up herbs and nuts, so get the fuck out of your basic basil bullshit. You can use cilantro, parsley, spinach, kale, or a little bit of everything together and that shit is still a pesto. Sub out the almonds for walnuts, pine nuts, peanuts, what the fuck ever. Here's a classic basil pesto recipe, but feel free to substitute your ass off with any of these ingredients.

>> **Makes about 1¼ cups**

2½ cups packed torn basil leaves or whatever herb/green combo you're going for

⅔ cup slivered or sliced almonds or other nut

2 cloves garlic, chopped

1 teaspoon grated lemon zest

¼ cup olive oil

¼ cup water

2 tablespoons lemon juice

¾ teaspoon salt

BASIL PESTO

Put all the ingredients in a food processor and blend until smooth-ish. No food processor? Calm the fuck down. Just put the nuts in a plastic bag and smash them until they're tiny and chop the rest of that shit up super small too. Mix all of it together with a fork until it looks like a paste.

If you're pressed for time, you can prep this shit a day ahead and keep it in the fridge for dinner tomorrow.

TOFU RICOTTA

>> **Makes about 2 cups**

¼ cup raw sunflower seeds

1 block (14 ounces) extra-firm tofu*

2 tablespoons olive oil

½ teaspoon grated lemon zest

1 tablespoon lemon juice

¼ teaspoon salt

3 to 4 cloves garlic, minced

¼ cup nooch*

1 Add the sunflower seeds to a food processor and run that motherfucker until everything is in tiny pieces. Take the tofu out of the package and squeeze out as much water as you can. Add the tofu to the food processor and run it until it's all mixed in with the sunflower seeds.

2 Dump the tofu mixture into a bowl and stir in the olive oil, lemon zest, lemon juice, salt, and garlic. Sprinkle in the nooch. Done and done. Throw in the fridge until you're ready for it.

* WTF? See page 189.

DID YOU KNOW?

There are security checkpoints as you enter the state of California that confiscate smuggled food. We make everybody share here SO BRING ENOUGH FOR THE WHOLE CLASS.

3 tablespoons olive oil

1½ cups panko bread crumbs*

1 teaspoon grated lemon zest

¼ teaspoon garlic powder

¼ teaspoon paprika

¼ teaspoon salt

This crunchy son of a bitch improves anything you pour it on top of. It's been our obsession for the last year. Now make it yours.

PANKO PASTA TOPPING

In a medium skillet, warm the olive oil over medium-low heat. Add the panko and stir that shit around so everything gets some oil on it. Keep stirring until it starts to look a little golden, 3 to 5 minutes depending on however hot you personally consider is medium-low heat. Sometimes people just read "HEAT" and fucking crank their stoves. ANYWAYS, stir in the lemon zest, garlic powder, paprika, and salt until it's all mixed in. Then turn off the heat and pour the topping onto a plate. Use right away or let it cool before storing. This tasty topping will keep for 2 weeks stored in an airtight container in the fridge.

1 cup sliced almonds

½ cup nooch*

¼ cup flour**

1 tablespoon garlic powder

½ teaspoon grated lemon zest

½ teaspoon salt

Everyone's got that shaker with the green lid in their fridge with a label older than you. Take a goddamn minute and blend up these ingredients to certify the freshness yourself.

60-SECOND PARM

Throw everything in a food processor or blender and run that shit until everything is reduced to crumbs. Throw it in an airtight jar and keep it in your fridge for up to 3 weeks.

WTF? See page 189.

** All-purpose, rice flour, whatever. This just keeps it from getting too sticky.

THANKS

To the one and only Phoenix for existing in all her glory and running the tightest security a kitchen has ever had; Clementine and Kamala for putting fur on everything; VJ and Rebecca for being on Team TK from the jump; to Nick Smith for always losing his fucking mind with us in the kitchen for all these books; Juliet for keeping shit straight while we kept focused(ish); Ian, Megan, and Flag for being chill neighbors and all around badass people; to Mick for dragging the taco cart across the desert.

And none of this could've been possible without the crew at Rodale—Gail, Dervla, Jeff, Rae Ann, Yelena, Aly, Susan, Mary Ann, Angie, Marilyn, Kate, and Anna—Lauren for handling shit so we don't have to, along with Richard, and Kim at Inkwell; Sally at Stroock for the muscle; the whole crew at UTA; Hayley for the style and stupid jokes. And last but not least Nick Wagner, whose amazing illustrations and art direction makes all of our books worth looking at. Thanks to all y'all for your hard work, early mornings, late nights, infinite patience, well-placed GIFs, and relentless enthusiasm. We owe y'all drinks or weed. Your choice.

And to our audience who've shared posts, liked photos, cooked our food, or spent your hard-earned cash on the things we've created. We're humbled to have the opportunity to make y'all laugh and be in your kitchens over these past few years. We'll do it forever if you let us. We never imagined having a job or a life like we do now and we appreciate every last one of you who supports us. We're lucky as fuck to have you on our team and we know it. Thank you.

—MICHELLE AND MATT

ICON INDEX

GENERAL INDEX

Underscored page references indicate sidebars. **Boldface** references indicate photographs.

D

Desserts
  Almond Cake with Peach Caramel, 162–63
  Banana Chocolate Chip Cookies, **164**, 165
  Brown Sugar Blueberry Polenta Scones, 158, **159**
  Cinnamon Kettle Corn, 179
  Coconut Pralines, **176**, 177
  Creamsicles, 166
  Jasmine Rice Pudding, **170**, 171
  Nana's Chocolate Crunch No-Bake Cookies, 174
  Puppy Chow, 178
  Snickerdoodles, **160**, 161
  Sweet Sugar Glaze, 167, **168**
  Tahini Fudge, 172, **173**
  Wine Cake, 167, **168**
Dill
  Greek Orzo Salad, 51
  Protein-Packed Mixed Herb Tabbouleh Salad, 50
  Shredded Apple Polenta with Dill, 125
Dining out, x, xii–xiii
Doubling recipes, 58

E

Eggplant
  Curry Roasted Eggplant, 8, **9**
Excuse for not cooking, ix–x, xvi

F

Falafel
  Clean-Out-the-Fridge Falafel, 107
Fast-food restaurants, x, xii, xiii
Fattoush, 44, **45**
Fennel
  Arugula Potato Salad with Fennel, 31
  Crispy Fennel, 13, **13**
  Winter Veggie Slaw with Caramelized Shallot Dressing, 42
Fideo, 108
Flautas
  Flautas for Every Meal, 6

Freezing homemade meals, 58
Frozen ingredients, vs. frozen meals 72
Fruits. *See also specific fruits*
  Whateverthefuck Fruit Smoothie, 137
Fudge
  Tahini Fudge, 172, **173**

G

Garam masala, 188
  One-Pot Chickpea Biryani, **94**, 95
Garlic, roasting, 187, **187**
Gin
  Malhotra Muddle, 142, **143**
Ginger
  Ginger Curry Noodle Soup, **76**, 77
  Malhotra Muddle, 142, **143**
Ginger ale
  Amber Waves, **148**, 149
  Ginger Fizz, 150
  Malhotra Muddle, 142, **143**
Ginger beer
  Amber Waves, **148**, 149
  Ginger Fizz, 150
  Malhotra Muddle, 142, **143**
Glaze
  Sweet Sugar Glaze, 167, **168**
Grains. *See also specific grains*
  for building salad bowl, 46
  cooking guidelines for, 182–83
  Hippie Dippie Salad Bowls, **40**, 41
Green beans
  One-Pot Chickpea Biryani, **94**, 95

H

Hatch chiles
  Chickpea and Green Chile Soup, 70, **71**
  Hatch Chile Salsa, **20**, 22
Health, food influencing, x, xiii, xv, xvi
Herbs. *See also specific herbs*
  dried, for pantry, 190
Home cooking, benefits of, xv

Hot sauce
  Apollo's Fury, 132, **133**
  Creamy Squash Mac and Cheese with Hot Sauce Bread Crumbs, 90–91, **91**

I

Icons, recipe, xx, 208–209
Ingredients
  for cutting corners, 98
  shopping for, xv
  stocking, for recipes, xx

J

Jalapeños. *See also* Chipotles in adobo sauce
  Borracho Squash and Bean Burritos, 104, **105**
  Chickpea and Green Chile Soup, 70, **71**
  Hatch Chile Salsa, **20**, 22
  Jalapeño-Cilantro Dressing, 28
  Nachos with Tex-Mex Queso, **123**, 124
  Pineapple Salsa, **20**, 21
  Quinoa Taco Mix, **120**, 122
  Skillet Beer Chili Mac, 87, **88**
  Southwestern Pasta Salad, 43
Japchae, **112**, 113
Jicama
  Firecracker Salad, 28, **29**
  Jicama-Corn Salsa, **20**, 22

K

Kalamata olives
  Arugula Potato Salad with Fennel, 31
  French Crushed Chickpea and Artichoke Heart Salad, 38, **39**
  Polenta Puttanesca, 117, **118**
  Swiss Chard and Tomato Linguine with Balsamic-Glazed Chickpeas, 100–101
Kale
  All-Purpose Veggie Soup, 79
  Chipotle Caesar Salad, 32, **33**

motherfuckin fin